I'M ANYMORE!

Mary, My Mother, Help Me to see God's Love for Me Today

by Father Patrick A. Martin

Father Patrick A. Martin
11510 Windtree
San Antonio, TX 78253

(207) 423-4774
fatherpat@runbox.com

Program Scheduler: Mrs. Patricia Kozar
(210) 679-8434
kozpat69@gmail.com

Website: www.fatherpatrickmartin.com

First published by Dog Ear Publishing
4011 Vincennes Road
Indianapolis, IN 46268
www.dogearpublishing.net

ISBN: 978-145756-786-5

This book is printed on acid-free paper.
Printed in the United States of America

CONTENTS

DEDICATION

This book is dedicated to my worldwide family, whose loving prayers have helped me to see God's love in my life and ministry.

FOREWORD

by Deacon Jerome and Patricia Kozar

It is our honor and privilege to write the foreword to Father Patrick A. Martin's sixth book regarding his life experiences and the significant impact the Rosary has had on his life.

Fr. Pat was introduced to me (Jerry) at our wedding in 1965, and of course, his sister Patricia met her brother Patrick shortly after her birth. Through the years, with our military service life, remarkably, our paths crossed many times. We were there with our three-month-old son, Andrew, when Fr. Pat took his final vows as Brother Pat in 1969. We were able to visit Fr. Pat at Walsh College in Ohio as we were traveling across the country to our next assignment. We were able to be with Brother Pat during our assignment in Washington, D.C., when he was attending

Catholic University, and during the period, he became the godfather to our second son, Julian. We have been blessed with multiple visits from him over the years here in our retirement city of San Antonio, Texas. The latest thing was Fr. Pat being the primary celebrant at our fiftieth wedding anniversary in 2015. Of course, we would be remiss if we didn't mention our daughter Jennifer, who always said that Fr. Pat was her favorite uncle, and he has emphatically stated that she is his favorite niece. As you will read in this book, he now is very much a part of our family.

We love him dearly, and we thank God that through all these years, our relationship and love has grown to one of a family of God.

Deacon Jerome P. (Jerry) Kozar
Patricia N. (Martin) Kozar

INTRODUCTION

Ave Maria Place is no more. Awildcanary.com is no more. Fr. Pat, because of illness, is now retired. But guess what? *God isn't done with him!*

Can you believe that my sixth book is finally in your loving hands? The book has come to you from my retirement home in San Antonio, Texas. With God, there is no such thing as retirement. He's always got something for us to do. I've preached about a dozen missions since retiring, and the requests don't stop coming in. The beginnings of this book have sat in my computer for about three years, and suddenly, he said it was time to finish it! And so, here it is. Writing this book has been a real healing experience for me. I pray it may be the same for you! Thank you for your almost infinite patience in waiting for it! Hopefully, you'll find it was worth waiting for! God bless you and all whose love and gifts have made this possible.

Gratefully always,

Fr. Pat

1 HELP!

"Look at blind Brother Pat" many a New York City rehab counselor said to his audience in the early 1970s. "He's truly independent. He travels all over the city all by himself. He needs no help. What an example!"

"He needs no help ..." How accurately those counselors summarized my life at that time. Handicapped since 1953, I had seen the goal of my life to be "needing no help"! I had watched brothers and sisters grow up and become independent ... I had watched school classmates on that same road ... From my earliest days after the meningitis of 1953, my constant yearning was to be just like them— to need no help. How exciting it was when I was finally allowed to walk home from school all alone, instead of waiting for the school bus! I hated needing extra help at school. I wanted so much to be just like everyone else ...

Was that wish to need no one's help the biggest part of my excitement in being accepted at the ripe old age of sixteen to enter the Brothers of Christian Instruction Juniorate? And was it not that same wish that stopped me from giving in to extreme homesickness at the boarding school, made me dare to play sports at the school, stopped me from telling the Brothers that I was blind? I wanted so much to be just like everyone else—who needed no help!

Many years later, August 19, 2016, was an ordinary traveling day for me. After bidding an early morning "Goodbye!" to my sister Patricia, I got in the car with my brother-in-law Deacon Jerome Kozar and headed for the San Antonio Airport. As always, we began our half-hour trip with the Rosary, asking Mary at each decade, "Help us see God's love for us today."

My flights that day took me from San Antonio to Atlanta and from Atlanta to Ashville, North Carolina. Delta had dutifully provided a wheelchair help at each airport. In Ashville, we had proceeded just past security when I heard laughing voices calling out, "Paging Father Pat!" Ray and Marie Young were there to pick me up for their church's parish mission on God's love in our broken lives. What an exciting reunion it was right there in the Ashville Airport!

The drive from Ashville to Ray and Marie's summer home in Hayesville in the Smokey Mountains was about three hours. We used every minute of the drive catching up! I've known Ray and Marie since the early 1990s when I first met them at a mission in their home parish, Holy Name of Jesus, Indialantic, Florida. I've lost count of the times we've gotten together since then. Now we would be together for almost three weeks! They had talked to their North Carolina pastor, Father Alex, and he had invited me to come to his two parishes: IHM, Hayesville, and St. Williams, Murphy, North Carolina. Ray and Marie had also talked to another priest friend, Father Juan, in nearby Georgia, and so a third mission had been booked for his St. Francis parish!

Ray and Marie Young's "summer home" was a small cabin in the Smokey Mountains. Would I mind staying with them there during the mission days, they asked? That stay has been a little corner of Heaven for me!

"Mary, help me to see God's love for me today," I had prayed with my brother-in-law early that morning. I've prayed that little prayer daily for more than thirty-nine years now, and I'm still amazed at the ways that Mother Mary finds to help me see her son's love for me brand new each day! I no sooner stepped into Ray and Marie's cabin in the mountains than I knew exactly why I was there! I would have two breaks between the three parish missions … It was time to write my book! I had begun writing my sixth book a year and a half earlier … It sat unfinished on my MacBook! By the end of my first mission break, the book was well on its way!

I thank my sister and brother-in-law, Pat and Jerry Kozar of San Antonio, who gave me the space and encouragement to begin writing again, and a dear friend, Mary Chaffin, also of San Antonio, who has read this manuscript over and over again as it's grown to maturity! And how do I thank properly my dear Ray and Marie for their little cabin in the Smokey Mountains and their inspiring love that has nurtured this writing? Wow!! My dearest sister and brother-in-law have added the finishing flourish to the book with their loving "Foreword." And then there are all of the book's dear sponsors, without whom the book would never have been! How grateful I am for all the help that gives this now finished book to you!

Help? Those New York City rehab counselors would find it difficult to believe that the same independent young man they had praised so highly in the early 1970s was now authoring a book on his needing help! Was this really the same young man? How had he changed so radically?

2 "GOLDEN ROSE"

September 12, 2000, will always be a special day in my memory. It was the thirty-first anniversary of my father's death, but even more, it was my visit to the Shrine of Our Lady of Knock in Ireland! This was my second mission journey through Ireland, and I had made only one special request of those who had organized the whole trip, to prayerfully visit that special shrine. How exciting it was that morning when Paul, my driver for much of the mission journey, announced that we were going to Knock that day and there, I would get to celebrate Mass at the very gable where Our Lady had appeared in 1879!

I've now returned to Ireland for missions several times since my first trip in 1998. My favorite spot in that dear land is the Shrine of Our Lady of Knock. The story of Our

Lady's apparition there touched my heart so dearly, perhaps because it was so much like our own stories.

In the early 1800s, the people of Ireland were suffering grievously. They had been over-run, and their best lands had been taken from them. The potato famine of the mid-1800s had caused countless deaths and untold suffering. It was in the midst of that suffering that the Mother of God appeared in the poorest part of that land, bringing unconquerable hope in the midst of their sufferings. Seventeen people— young and old, educated and uneducated—saw the lighted gable wall from miles away and traveled on foot to see what it might be. The scene, which remained on the gable wall for hours, was brilliant. Mary was there with St. Joseph on her one side and the Apostle John on her other side. John was holding the book of the Gospels, and it was said that the very words of the open book could be read by the onlookers. In front of the three of them was the Altar of Sacrifice, and on the altar was the Lamb of God glorified. Not a word was spoken from the scene on the gable wall as the people watched in silence. As the vision gradually faded, the witnesses were awestruck. It had been raining all the while they had traveled to the site and all the hours that they had stood there in silent prayer. As the scene faded, however, they all realized that, standing there in the rain, none of them were wet! News of the apparition spread quickly throughout the land. Nothing changed for the land or its people, except now discouragement was gone, and hope was alive!

As I visited the gravesites of the seventeen who had been there that special day, I prayed only for that same hope that would carry me through whatever storms and sufferings this world would dump upon me!

On my latest mission through Ireland, the mission attendees filled my heart with tears of joy as they sang every night my truly favorite Marian hymn, the story of Our Lady of Knock, by Dana Rosemary Scallon:

"Golden Rose"

Golden Rose, Queen of Ireland,

all my cares and troubles cease

as we kneel with love before you,

Lady of Knock, my Queen of Peace.

There were people of all ages

gather 'round the gable wall,

poor and humble men and women,

little children that you called.

We are gathered here before you,

and our hearts are just the same,

filled with joy at such a vision

as we praise your name.

Golden Rose, Queen of Ireland,

all my cares and troubles cease

as we kneel with love before you,

Lady of Knock, my Queen of Peace.

Though your message was unspoken,

still the truth in silence lies

as we gaze upon your vision

and the truth I try to find.

Here I stand with John the teacher

and with Joseph at your side,

and I see the Lamb of God

on the Altar glorified.

Golden Rose, Queen of Ireland,

all my cares and troubles cease

as we kneel with love before you,

Lady of Knock, my Queen of Peace.

And the Lamb will conquer,

and the Woman clothed in the sun

will shine Her light on everyone.

Yes, the Lamb will conquer,

and the Woman clothed in the sun

will shine Her light on everyone.

Golden Rose, Queen of Ireland,

all my cares and troubles cease

as we kneel with love before you,

Lady of Knock, my Queen of Peace.

So many people today point to the presence of suffering, destruction, disease, persecution, etc. as their justification for not believing in God. How many from my youth questioned my faith, pointing out that I was still blind? They assumed that Jesus was supposed to take away suffering. Is he not? I reminded them that Jesus didn't heal all the blind, all the lepers, all the paralyzed … of Israel. He didn't even get rid of his own sufferings. He came not to take away suffering but to help us in our sufferings, to redeem it! He came to bring hope to a suffering world.

3 MY MINISTRY? OR, HIS MINISTRY?

"Can I help you up?" the New York City cab driver asked as I lay there on the cobblestone pavement at 620 East 20th Street. I had just arrived in New York City from San Antonio, Texas, beginning a three-week tour of my ministry's roots. In September, 1970, the city of New York had hired me to find the disabled and help them to find the library services that too many of them weren't enjoying only because they knew nothing about those services. My work quickly spread far beyond the city's boundaries, however, and ultimately brought me to the diocese of Norwich, Connecticut, where, with a special permission from His Holiness (now Blessed) Pope Paul VI, I was ordained a blind priest by the Most Reverend Daniel P. Reilly in 1978 to bring the services of the Church to those who could not come to the Church. For years since, I had gone from Norwich to parishes all over the world, preaching the good news of God's helping love to the suffering of this world.

My 2016 trip to the northeast US was exciting, bringing me back to the ministry's very beginnings and its people. That pilgrimage hadn't even begun, however, when I had tripped getting out of the cab and found myself lying there on the cobblestone pavement on East 20th Street. My cab driver couldn't have been more kind or helpful. He picked up my white cane and the gift I had brought and helped me over to the level, smooth sidewalk where I found my balance again. I thanked him profusely.

With my blindness and other disabilities, I have traveled all over this world. My own disabilities have most often been my invitation to bring the good news of God's love to others just like myself. But now, recovering from my fall, I found my mind traveling faster and farther than my broken body had ever gone by trains, buses, or planes. I quickly imagined myself back in places all over, where I had been told how foolish it was for me to travel as I did: "With your disabilities you could retire and not put yourself through all the aggravation of travel, airports, train stations, inaccessible churches, schools, etc. You could settle down and take care of yourself. What's going to happen if you have an accident or such on one of these trips?"

I wasn't hurt physically at all from my fall, but my pride was badly bruised. I found myself agreeing readily with my "advisers" that yes, it was downright stupid and unsafe for me to be traveling as I have for years and years now. In those few depressing moments, I found myself rehearsing how I would tell the family I was about to visit, as well as all those others on my three-week itinerary, that my traveling work was truly now finished. I would sit at home and write, etc., but no more travels …

God didn't let my pity party go on too long, however. It was suddenly as if he had slapped me upside the head, and then he spoke: "Patrick," he asked, not really expecting and answer from me. "Who is doing all this work? Is it you or me? Did you choose this work? Or did I choose you? Who are you even to think of quitting? When I chose you, Patrick, I knew how disabled you were, and yes, I knew how further disabled you'd become in the future! And I still chose you to do this work! It's not your work, Patrick! So it's not yours to quit! It's my work ,and if I want to choose a blind, physically disabled, hearing-impaired person for my work, that's my business …"

Wow! Wonder of wonders! In the briefest of moments, I had gone from tripping on the street to being helped so kindly by my cab driver, and from a self-pity party to a fantastic recommitment—not to my work but to God's work! I never said a word to the family that night about my happening on the street, and the rest of my three-week itinerary became a wonderful retreat for me, witnessing daily God's redeeming, helping love in my broken life.

From New York, I traveled to Stafford Springs, Connecticut, and then on to Willimantic, Connecticut. And from Connecticut, I moved to St. Anthony's parish in North Providence, Rhode Island, for a four-day mission on God's love in our broken lives. After visiting dozens of ministry family and friends in New York, Connecticut, and Rhode Island, I moved on to Massachusetts and Maine for other families, growing with each visit in my awareness of God's redeeming, helping love for me. Then I flew home to San Antonio, Texas.

What a fantastic retreat those three weeks were for me. I left San Antonio as the ministry director going up to visit all those fantastic volunteers who've worked with me for years and years now. I returned as the much beloved one who was so dearly visited on the journey by the one who has so fantastically chosen the likes of broken me for his work! The most fantastic revelation of the retreat was that this is not my work—it's not my ministry . . . From the very beginnings, this truly has been God's work, not mine. And it still is his work!

How is it that I could even think that this was my work? How quickly I can forget all the wonders of his calling in my life and ministry!!! Just think of all the miracles of my life: recovering from TB meningitis all the way to being ordained a blind priest! Just think of the countless miracles of God's love that I've now experienced in my more than seventy-four years! It's so easy to take all these miracles for granted and begin living as if I'm doing something for God instead of bowing in humble adoration before the one who does everything for me and for all his people!

And God's loving care and guidance never stops. I was so busy with my pity party there on East 20th Street in New York City that I didn't even "see" his special helper of love, that dearest of cab drivers, that God had so lovingly sent to care for me. Instead of rushing off to look for his next fare, he got out of his cab, picked me up, made sure I wasn't seriously hurt, picked up my belongings for me, and led me to where I felt secure again! I wonder today, How many, many, many of God's "helpers of love" have I missed in my life because I presumed I already knew his love? Because I was too busy to even notice his love for me today? Because I was sure I already knew his love? Because I was satisfied with the ways I've seen his love in my past? Because I thought I didn't really need help in seeing his love?

4 THE ROSARY

Ash Wednesday 1979 was without doubt the most eventful Ash Wednesday of my seventy-four years of life! No, it wasn't a day of great sacrifice on my part, a day of great fervor in service and prayer, a day of love and turning to God ... It was a day of crippling anger and discouragement for me. My ministry for the handicapped was falling apart right before my eyes! I had been ordained a priest just six months before, and now I found myself wishing with all my heart that I could just run away somewhere where nobody knew me, where nobody could ever know me ...

Ash Wednesday 1979 was not an exciting day for me at all. It was the opposite. I had returned from a preaching journey the night before, finding my home ministry in shambles. Donations, which kept our ministry alive, had mysteriously stopped coming in. We were getting deeper and deeper in debt. In 1972 when my bosses at the city of New York had said no to my ministry outreach work from the library, my superior with the Brothers of Christian Instruction, Brother Francis Blouin, had challenged me to leave the city's employment and work freelance, depending on the good Lord for my daily sustenance instead of upon the city. "The city won't pay you to do God's work," he had said. And so, my Divine Providence ministry was begun. I never quite got used to the almost incredible miracles of God's providing for all my daily needs. During those years, I had no bills that weren't able to be paid on time. It was shortly thereafter that Bishop Daniel Reilly invited me to found a ministry for the handicapped for his Diocese of Norwich. I had asked and received his permission to operate the new ministry "on Divine Providence," trusting in God for the ministry's daily sustenance, as I had now for several years.

Trusting in God is a fantastic walk with the God who loves me, but I learned that, sadly, it's not a walk I can demand of others. God hadn't demanded it of me. He had challenged, inspired, and enticed me, but he had never forced me to go his way. "The ministry should be run as a business," people argued. "Borrow what we need. Make appropriate charges for services and items to pay bills ..." Divine Providence was just not the way to run a business ...

My heart was sick as I returned home that Ash Wednesday. I was angry. I was depressed. "I don't even know what to do for Lent this year," I said angrily in my prayer that morning. I was shocked, utterly amazed, by the answer that came immediately from God: "Pick up the Rosary that you haven't prayed in sixteen years," he said, "and make that your Lenten penance. Instead of giving up something this Lent, do something." It just totally amazed me that the God to whom I talked in prayer would talk back to me!

"What's that going to do?" I answered immediately. I had thrown away the practice of the daily Rosary years and years ago. It was just all repetition, empty mumbling. Wasn't it better for me to talk to God in my own words? And why go through Mary? Couldn't I talk directly to Jesus? And what's the Rosary got to do with all my ministry troubles anyway? I questioned all of this. I also wondered, How is the Rosary going to help anything?

"You won't know until you try it" was his clear, unmistakable answer. He didn't argue with any of my Rosary objections. He simply went on, "Pray your Rosary first thing in the morning, and ask my mother at the beginning of each decade, 'Help me to see God's love for me today.' That will bring your mind back if it's wandered during the previous decade."

He didn't argue, but I did! "I'm a nighttime person," I said. "Wouldn't it be just as good to pray at night as early in the morning? I love praying at night," I went on, "when the day's business and activities are quieted down."

He responded immediately, "Do your friends put gas in the car at the beginning of a trip or at the end?"

I argued on, "Shouldn't I at least be praying to love you more? Praying to see your love for me just sounds so selfish."

He didn't even answer. I had no more arguments. The discussion was over.

The morning Rosary, praying for our Mother Mary's help to see God's love for me that day, was probably the most difficult Lenten penance I've ever had. I was so tempted every morning at the beginning of that Lent to quit. The prayer just sounded so selfish, and I really couldn't see that any good could ever come from it. And the ministry problems certainly weren't getting any better. Our cash flow was all but nonexistent. But what truly intrigued me was that the whole idea had not been mine! Praying the Rosary, let alone the morning Rosary, had most assuredly not been my idea at all! And praying the Rosary *to ask for help* had most assuredly not been my idea either. And so I decided I would go on with the penance to the end of Lent. It certainly would do me no harm.

The first few weeks of my Lenten penance were indeed difficult, but very quietly things began to happen without my planning or realizing. The ministry troubles got no better; in fact, they got worse. Incredibly, however, those ministry troubles controlled my peace less and less! I never even realized what was happening as those weeks of Lent passed by.

I think it was sometime during the fifth week of Lent when I got the most beautiful glimpse of what was happening inside me that Lent. I got up that morning "on the wrong side of the bed," as my dad used to call it. Scientists say it's probably a puddle of chemicals that's off-kilter in the brain. Whatever it was, I got up that morning in a real bad mood. God help the first one who would cross my path that day! It wouldn't be a pleasant crossing! But because I had been praying my morning Rosary for those several weeks, I picked it up immediately and began to pray, as always, "Mary, help me to see God's love for me today!"

In the middle of the Rosary's last decade that morning, I began to cry. My mood, I suddenly realized, had changed completely in those few minutes of prayer! I blurted out through my tears, "Who did you spare from the venom of my tongue this morning by getting me to pray this way? Who would have been sliced to ribbons by my tongue had I gone out into the world in that mood that was mine when I first awoke this morning? But who now won't be hurt at all today because you got me to pray this way?"

That Ash Wednesday of 1979, God hadn't told me why I should pray the Rosary every morning that Lent. He had just said, "*Pray!*" Now I had a dear glimpse of *why*!

On Easter Sunday, that glimpse was developed into a full-blown photo! My ministry's troubles had only gotten worse as the weeks and months had gone by. Strangely now, however, I had a peace that the troubles couldn't destroy. At Easter that year, I knew I was hooked. I couldn't quit praying with every morning's Rosary, "Mary, help me to see God's love for me today!"The following June, my bishop decided that the ministry should be dissolved and refounded brand-new.

That May, I had three "missions" to preach: one in Ohio and two in Michigan. I usually don't make deals with God, but I did at that time. I used a credit card to pay for all of those travels and begged the Lord to pay it off completely … After the Ohio mission, the mission offerings were simply put in a sack and handed to me. I threw the sack into my suitcase and moved on to my first Michigan mission. Those offerings were placed with the Ohio missions, and I moved on to my final mission stop. I held my breath at the end of that mission when the pastor brought out the offerings basket and asked for my airline tickets. "There's a priest here," I said, "who came down from his diocese in Canada to learn about this mission, to bring it back to his own broken people. I would like to take care of his expenses first." The pastor argued, looking at the basket's meager contents, that he'd rather take care of mine first. Then I opened my suitcase and added the offerings from my two previous missions to his basket. He relaxed.

After taking care of the Canadian priest's expenses, the pastor asked, "Now can I have your tickets?" I then pointed out three disabled students who had come from the University of Michigan to learn the retreat and bring it back to their University Newman Center. The pastor knew arguing with me was useless. When the students' expenses were cared for, he said, "Now, can I have your tickets?"

"One last thing first," I said. "Let's take out $100 and put it in a coffee can for handicapped get-togethers in your parish in the future." After that, I handed over my tickets and cried tears of fantastic joy as the pastor counted what was left in the basket and matched it exactly with my ticket expenses, penny for penny! "Did you know this was going to happen?" the pastor asked in utter amazement. "No," I cried, "but I prayed with all my heart that it would!" Sharing my mission journey with my bishop that June, he readily agreed that the newly refounded ministry could live on Divine Providence!

A year or so after the Norwich ministry was refounded, I met my dear bishop on the sidewalk. After exchanging pleasant greetings, he asked me, "Patrick, how did you get through that year from hell?" I was amazed at his description of that year of intense suffering. His description was right on! I reached into my pocket and pulled out my Rosary. Holding it in my hands, I told him the story of my Lent of 1979, the Lent that had changed my life! "I don't think that my morning Rosary did much for my ministry," I said, "but it sure did a lot for me! It gave me a peace that the ministry troubles couldn't touch." I can still "see" the tears on my bishop's cheeks as he responded, "I hope you never quit that morning Rosary!"

It's now more than three dozen years since that dear Lent of 1979, and no matter where I am or what's going on in my life, my day still begins with that morning Rosary: "Mary, help me to see God's love for me today!"

5 MARY?

People often tell me, "Father Pat, I don't have to pray for help to see God's love in my life. I see his love all through my life. If you only knew the things he's done for me!"

"But that's all in the past," I say to them after hearing their wonderful litany of love gifts from God in their life. "Have you seen his love for you today? This hour? This moment?"

Others ask, "Father Pat, you've prayed all these years for help to see God's love for you today. You must really know his love for you by now, no?"

I always respond, "I have had many glimpses of God's love for me in the past, but every day that I ask, I see his love for me in some brand-new way!" I am truly excited each morning as I ask Mother Mary on waking up, "Mary, help me to see God's love for me today!"

And what a gift it is for me to be asking the Blessed Virgin Mary to help me to see God's love for me today! In the fall of 1963, as a young novice Brother of Christian Instruction, I had quite literally thrown her out of my life and my spirituality. I had objected to the young Brothers having to make the public "Consecration" to Mary during our novitiate year, arguing that we could go directly to Jesus. After all, we were adults, preparing to dedicate our lives to the service of Jesus. Did we really need the help of a mommy? I had left the Blessed Virgin Mary out of my life for some fifteen years or so.

Then, in November, 1978, I was asked to lead a retreat for the handicapped in Sault Ste. Marie, Ontario, Canada. It was my first retreat as "Father Pat." It was an incredible weekend retreat, with more than eighty retreatants from all over the Sault Ste. Marie area. Getting to celebrate the Sacraments for the first time with my fellow suffering brothers and sisters brought me more joy than I could have ever imagined. I knelt beside my bed at the end of the retreat, thanking God for the wonders of his love that had been so evident during the entire weekend. All of a sudden as I knelt there, however, I beheld the Cross of Jesus right there before my blind eyes! Jesus was hanging alive on that Cross, and standing beneath was his Mother Mary and, not John, the disciple Jesus loved, but *me*!

In utter disbelief I gazed in silence at the scene. Then I heard Jesus speak to his mother, "Behold, your son." My silent awe continued as he then turned to me and said, "Behold, your mother." I was not at all prepared for the words that I then heard come from my own mouth there beneath the Cross of Jesus: "Who needs her?" I heard myself bellow in the face of Jesus. "I don't need a mommy. Can't I go directly to you, Jesus?" Mary just looked at me in silence. Jesus didn't answer. And then the scene was gone …

I leaned over on my bed and began to cry almost convulsively. I begged God for hours that night that he would offer her to me just once more. I promised with all my heart that I wouldn't demand to know why. I would stomp on my pride and simply accept the gift of Mary from him on the Cross. "Please," I tearfully pleaded for hours that night. But the scene never came back. I cried myself to sleep …

In the morning I awoke with a horrible headache and a nauseous stomach, probably from crying all night. Visiting with the priest whose parish had hosted the retreat, I asked him to pray over me that I might feel well enough to fly home the next morning. He instructed me to sit in the stuffed living room chair and then called those who were there visiting with us to gather around me and pray with us. Knowing nothing of my lack of devotion to Mary over the years, he began, with arms outstretched toward me, to describe the very details of each of my life's Mary-rejecting moments! As he prayed my "confession," I cried more tears than I knew I had. When he finished, he asked the mother of the family there, "Hug him now, as Mary would hug him!" And as she hugged, he gave me absolution for all my rejecting life.

Oh, what a gift! What an unexpected, undeserved gift that confession was! Mary was truly home in my heart after that confession-prayer time that morning—more at home than I had ever known her. But that priest, giving me that beautiful absolution, never thought to pray for my head and my stomach at all. They were at least as hurting when he finished his prayer as when he had begun it! That afternoon, I had been asked to go down to the hospital in town to pray with the chronically ill who hadn't been able to get out of the hospital for the retreat. I made up my mind that after I had prayed over the last patient, I would ask to be admitted to the hospital *as a patient*. I wasn't going to attempt to fly home the next morning feeling like I still did that afternoon.

As I moved from patient to patient, the only words that would come from my most unworthy lips were "Hail Mary, full of Grace! The Lord is with you! Blessed are you among women, and blessed is the fruit of your womb, Jesus! Holy Mary, Mother of God, pray for us sinners now and at the hour of our death! Amen!"

Patient after patient, that simple "Ave Maria" and my priestly blessing were the only words that would come from my mouth that afternoon. Finally, the hospital's director of pastoral care, with tears in her own eyes, turned to me and said, "That was the last patient. Now will you pray an 'Ave' over me and give me your blessing?"

As I honored her request, I cried. My head and my stomach were all better! While I had prayed for her kids, our Mother Mary had taken care of me, her spoiled, most undeserving one! I had thrown her out of my life for some fifteen years, and in an instant, she was at home in my heart! And now, Ash Wednesday 1979, barely six months after her dear homecoming, I was blessed with the Lenten challenge of the daily Rosary, praying for Mary's help to see God's love for me today! Wow! Wonder of wonders!

6 MARY, HELP ME TO SEE GOD'S LOVE FOR ME TODAY

When I first started, I had no idea what praying on waking up each morning for help to see God's love for me today would do for my life. That little prayer has actually turned my whole life upside down! It's actually changed the whole focus of my life. Instead of looking at what I'm doing for God—at what I'm supposed to be doing for God—I get up each morning now focusing on what he's doing for me! As a priest, I come to the altar now, not focused on what I am about to do for Jesus and his people, but rather, excited about what he's about to do for me and for his people!

It dawned on me some time after that first Lent how truly upside down my spiritual life had been for years and years. The Sacraments, I had learned as a child, were what God always did for me, never what I did for God. The very definition of a Sacrament that I had learned from the catechism in my youthful years put it so succinctly: "A Sacrament is an outward sign instituted by Christ to give us Grace." Nowhere in the definition did it talk about what I did for Christ, what I was supposed to do for him, how I was supposed to do it ... It only spoke of the Sacraments of gifts of his Grace for me. Wasn't it strange now, however, that my whole approach to the Sacraments was in terms of what I did for him and what I was supposed to do for him? For example, "I go to Communion ... I go to confession ..." I never even looked at all that he did for me! Wow! I truly had everything upside down. There's no area of my life that that little prayer—"Mary, help me to see God's love for me today"—hasn't touched and still continues to touch.

I have often told well-meaning healers that I really don't pray for the cure of my eyes. After all, it's my blindness, not sight, that's brought me all over the world. I've never asked to go anywhere, but requests have now brought me all over the English-speaking world to tell my suffering brothers and sisters of God's love. It's difficult for people to take in that I am truly a happy man, a happy blind man, that I really don't pray to change ...

Then, one morning, the good Lord had me listen carefully to the Rosary prayer he had given me in Lent of

1979: "Mary, my mother, help me to see God's love for me today." Suddenly, it was so obvious! I thought, *I do indeed pray every morning for the cure of my eyes, do I not? I'm praying to see God's love for me today, am I not?* But then, the good Lord corrected my thinking. I wasn't praying to see God's love for me; I was praying for Mary's help to see God's love for me! Big difference! I wasn't praying for the cure of my eyes that I might be able to see God's love on my own. I was praying to our Blessed Mother Mary to help me to see God's love for me today *with her eyes!* Wow!

Independence had been the name of my game for years and years now. I hated needing help, not being able to do this or that by myself. In my early New York days, I was so often held up by many a rehab counselor as the model for their clients: "Look at blind Brother Pat. He needs no help … He's a real success …" I delighted hearing people marvel at my traveling all over the city—indeed, all over the world—all by myself. When God taught me that Ash Wednesday morning to pray for his mother's help to see his love for me today, that was a real game changer, a total game changer for my life. I was actually asking for help, and I wasn't "all by myself!" It was not my life, my ministry, my work … It truly was *ours!* I wasn't alone anymore! Maybe, just maybe, God had called me to this work because I was blind and couldn't do everything all by myself? *I needed help!* My blindness made me need him, need his mother, and need his people. Wow!

7 HE REDEEMS MY LIFE FROM DESTRUCTION

Without doubt, the greatest gift that's come from my daily praying for Mary's help to see God's love for me today has been seeing his love "redeem my life from destruction." My favorite verse in the entire Bible has become Psalm 103's verse 4: "He redeems my life from destruction!" The Psalmist doesn't blame God for the destruction—doesn't say, "He gives me destruction in my life for this reason or that," or that he (God) permits it. The Psalmist says only, "He redeems my life from destruction!"

How well I remember that Saturday morning in 1954, playing with my brothers and sisters in our father's workshop while he was building some piece of furniture for a lady from town. I was ten years old and had gone blind the previous fall from meningitis. We kids were chasing each other around the woodpiles and posts in Daddy's shop when I suddenly smacked into a post. The blow smarted, and I began to cry. The lady stopped her instructions to my father and turned to me with words that astound me to this very day: "When you grow up," she said authoritatively, "you're going to see why God made you blind!"

Can you imagine telling a ten-year-old kid that it's God who made him blind, and then expecting him to fall madly, head-over-heels in love with that God? I'm not sure how many days or weeks later it was when God reached down and just took all that blaming from my heart with one of his dear "special helpers." Watching my dear mother putting all of us little ones to bed one night, it suddenly dawned on me that she wouldn't have made me blind. Could she be better than God? That lady in Dad's workshop who said that God had made me blind: Could God have given me a mother, a father who were better than he was? That lady herself wouldn't have made me blind, I was sure. Did she think she was better than God? People often ask me, "Father, how does God really talk to you? Do you hear his voice?" With our Blessed Mother's dear help, I see God and I hear his love in those he's brought into my life.

Without my really knowing it at all, my calling to preach God's love to this broken, suffering world was truly born that night. After that simple realization, I found myself bristling whenever I heard anyone blame God for suffering.

"Oh, God won't give you more than you can handle … Oh, I'm sure God has a reason for this … Oh, it's God's will …" I have no idea where or why suffering is in my life. Doctors had no idea where my meningitis came from or why it left me blind. But after realizing that night the goodness of the parents he gave me, I just knew in my ten-year-old heart that my sufferings in no way came from him. I didn't care where my sufferings came from; I just knew in my heart that they didn't come from him. "Come to me," Jesus said in Matthew 11:28, "all you who are weary and find this life burdensome, and I will give you rest!"

Praying for Mary's help to see God's love for me opens my blind eyes every day, looking for his love. That prayer has never grown old these more than thirty-nine years now. In times of difficulty, decisions, perils, pain, suffering … I now find myself praying that little prayer not only with my morning Rosary but often—very often—during those suffering days. Always, always, my suffering heart and soul find peace.

8 PEACE, GIFT OF MY MORNING ROSARY

Is there any gift like peace in the midst of this world's sufferings? Anyone can have peace when everything is going well. All the wealth and health this world can offer is empty if my heart and mind aren't filled with peace. When God challenged me that Ash Wednesday morning in 1979 to begin praying for help to see his love for me today, I had no idea the real gift that soon would be mine: the peace that the world, with all its pains and troubles, could not disturb—the peace that all my ministry troubles could not disturb. "Peace I leave with you; my peace I give to you. Not as the world gives do I give it to you. Do not let your hearts be troubled or afraid" (John 14:27).

Peace truly is God's gift to us. Humanity keeps trying to negotiate for peace, to bargain, to trade for peace …

and peace never comes. We've signed innumerable peace treaties. We've established the League of Nations and the United Nations. But we have less peace in our world today than before all these treaties and institutions! "Peace is my gift to you."

How do we find that peace that the world cannot disturb? In September 2001, after the horrible bombing of our World Trade Center, we were crippled with fear. There was no peace. At first, we didn't even know who the enemy was! All air traffic was halted completely for several days. "Is it going to happen again?" I had been giving a parish mission on God's love in our broken lives at Our Lady of the Valley parish in Donora, Pennsylvania, when 9/11 happened. Donora was only about fifty miles from where one of the bombing planes had come down. I had another mission scheduled for the next weekend on Long Island, New York. "I don't think I'm going to be able to get there this weekend," I said to the New York pastor on the phone. I explained that I was sitting in southwestern Pennsylvania, and no planes were flying, and all buses and trains were overbooked.

"I don't care if you walk," the pastor responded immediately. "Just get here!" He then explained that many of his parishioners worked at the World Trade Center, and at that point, they still had no idea how many of them had been killed. "We absolutely need the mission," he pleaded. I reassured him that somehow, I would indeed get there.

That Friday, September 14, the air-travel ban was lifted, and I made my way to Pittsburgh's airport. I was shocked to find less than a dozen fellow travelers on my flight to New York that morning! Many, many, many were just too afraid to fly, especially to New York. The flight attendant led me to my seat on that almost empty plane. "Father," she asked with a huge hug, "what gave you the courage to fly this morning?"

I had no idea what religion that flight attendant espoused, and I guess it really didn't matter. I reached into my pocket and took out my Rosary, explaining as I did how God had challenged me more than twenty years earlier to ask his mother's help every morning to see his love for me that day. "St. John tells us in his epistle that perfect love casts out all fear," I told her. "I don't have perfect love. You don't have perfect love. But the God who loves us does, indeed, have perfect love! Praying for daily help to see his love for me has quite literally taken fear out of my heart, even fear of terrorists! 'Amen, amen, I say to you, that you shall be sorrowful, but your sorrow shall be turned into joy.' "

"Mary, help me to see God's love for me today" is truly the prayer that has saved my life—perhaps saved my vocation? I often wonder if I would still be a priest today if God had not called me so dearly that Ash Wednesday in 1979. It's his love that I have been so privileged to see, with dear Mother Mary's help, that has brought me to this day, I am sure. And it's most assuredly his love that has made me the traveling missionary I am today.

9 AN OPEN DOOR

"Behold, I will set a door open before you which none will ever shut again" (Revelations 3:18). As I look at my praying for Mary's help to see God's love for me today, I see our Blessed Mother so often reaching down to open a door that's slammed shut in front of me! In my littleness, I couldn't even reach the doorknob, so she most lovingly reached it for me. She was always there in my life but, sadly, for many years I was just too blind, too proud, too independent to appreciate her, to need her.

In 1571 when Rome was about to be sacked by sea, His Holiness Pope Pius V called on the universal Church to pray the daily Rosary, asking Mary under the title of Our Lady of Victory to bring us her son's loving help and protection. Miraculously, the attacking fleet turned back on its course and the city was saved. Pope Pius V, thanking God for the victory, proclaimed October 7 to be the Church universal's feast of the Holy Rosary. Devotion to Mary for intercession with her son for protection and peace has grown steadily among the faithful throughout the world.

In my family, Mary was no stranger. During my five months in the hospital with meningitis in 1953, the family gathered daily to pray for me. The more my dear parents were discouraged and given absolutely no hope by the doctors, the more they prayed. When I came home from the hospital, those prayers didn't stop. I remember us leaving the evening dinner table before the dishes were cleaned up, and gathering in the living room to pray the Rosary. Dad or Mom would lead the prayers, and we would all respond. Many a Sunday afternoon, we would gather with others from the parish to celebrate the Benediction of the Blessed Sacrament and pray the Rosary together at the parish church.

The Rosary was no strange devotion for me. When I was seeking to find an open door to serving God, it was to our Blessed Mother Mary that I turned, and so often, it was her hand that opened the closed doors for me, I was sure. How had I let go of that dear guiding hand by the 1960s in my life? I was at Fordham University's charismatic prayer meeting on a Sunday evening in June 1972. A priest had just shared that he had felt an awful heavy burden on the prayer group for the last three weeks. He didn't know what the burden was, but begged us all to pray that God would relieve it, whatever it was. We all began to pray. Then a lady opened her Scriptures at random and read from St. Paul's letter to the Corinthians: "If one member suffers, the whole body groans in suffering with it." I started to weep, wondering if my bitterness against my provincial superior with the Brothers of Christian Instruction could be weighing down that entire prayer group, who knew nothing about it—indeed, the entire body of Christ. I had been with the Brothers since 1960 and, since 1970, had been working with the handicapped in New York City at the New York Public Library. My work with the suffering had quickly led me from spreading talking books among the city's handicapped to counseling and even "almost confessional" work with them. After talking with priests of my home diocese in Maine, I had decided to apply to enter the diocese as a seminarian, a candidate for the priesthood. I had been assured that if I were ordained a priest, I would have no parish; my parish would be the entire diocese, and my parishioners, the handicapped. It would be my calling to bring the Church to those who could not, or would not, come to it! Needless to say, I was one excited Brother of Christian Instruction as I sent off all my completed application papers. And then, my provincial superior stepped in and stopped everything in its tracks. I was called to be a Brother, not a priest, he said. I became one deeply embittered man when I got the diocese's letter telling me they couldn't accept me as a candidate over my superior's objections. He had closed the door in my face. Did he have more power than God, I wondered? And strangely, I don't remember praying to Our Lady at all during those days ...

In the heat of my struggles with the Brothers, a dear friend invited me to my first charismatic prayer meeting in the spring of 1972. After several prayer meetings, I was hooked. I looked forward each week to the Wednesday-night gatherings of priests, religious, and lay people, all gathered for prayer! I had then been invited to join the "core group," which gathered on Sunday nights as well. And so, there I was at my first core group meeting, finding myself melting down in tears! When I gained some control, I shared with the group my calling to serve my suffering brothers as a priest and how my provincial superior had stopped me dead in my tracks. Then I shared with them the anger and hatred that I had nursed against him ever since. Then I surprised myself with what I next shared with them: I begged them to pray that my heart of stone would be one day melted into a loving, pulsing, forgiving heart of flesh!

The priest who had first asked for the prayers that night now stood up. He was crying like I was as he said that in all of his priestly years, he had never heard a more beautiful confession. Could he give me absolution in community, as I had just confessed in community? I received the Sacrament of God's forgiving love that night like I had never received it in my life!

A lady came up to me at the end of the prayer that very special evening and handed me a slip of paper with the Biblical reference "Rev. 3:18" written on it. She said she didn't know what it was, but she was sure it would mean something to me. I cried and cried when I looked up the reference on getting home from the prayer meeting: "Behold I will set a door open before you which none will ever shut again." That little quote suddenly tied my whole life together! I seemed to be hearing that night that I wasn't to worry about that slammed door—he could, and he would, open it before me …

From the onset of my blindness, God's love has opened doors that seemed to be so firmly shut before me! When everyone else gave up on my life at the hospital in 1953, Doctor Warren and Nurse Lillian Skinner held the door to life open for me with their refusals to give up! When our hometown closed the door to public schooling because of my blindness, a fourth-grade teacher fought to get that door reopened for me. My superior with the Brothers truly became my dearest friend in the world! From being my staunchest roadblock on my priesthood road, he became my special helper, guiding and supporting me all along that road. Wow! Only God …

10 GOD'S LOVE FOR ME

"I didn't think you were going to make it there for a while," Bishop Daniel Patrick Reilly said so calmingly, so lovingly, to me as I knelt before him in the ceremony of my ordination to the priesthood on October 7, 1978. When His Holiness Pope Paul VI gave me special permission to be ordained as a blind priest, it was my dear bishop who had chosen my ordination date: the Feast of the Holy Rosary! Wow! When the entrance procession had brought me into St. Patrick's Cathedral in Norwich, Connecticut, a half hour earlier and I had discovered that the church was filled to overflowing with friends and family, I had been totally overwhelmed and had all but lost it! The reality that I was finally about to be ordained as a priest of God had suddenly hit me at that moment. My dear ordaining bishop had seen me so powerfully overcome at that moment and had wondered if he'd have to pick me up off the floor!

"How come you never got bitter when your ordination was canceled by Rome because of your blindness a year and a half ago?" a good priest friend asked me at the reception after my ordination Mass that morning. He and a hundred or so other priests had come to celebrate this day with me, a day that they and so many family and friends had thought realistically would never come. Most interestingly, anger had never been a part of my reaction when my ordination had been canceled because of my blindness the previous spring. My only reaction, I recall so clearly, had been fear—a deep fear that others would be driven away from the Church with bitterness because of the cancelation. What could I do? I had yearned to help them to believe as I did that God, who redeems our lives from destruction, would bring good, even out of this.

My life was filled with closed doors. Blinded from meningitis twenty-five years earlier, I had wasted too much time in discouragement and anger, standing before one closed door or another. Then I had observed with reverential awe how God's love had always provided "special helpers" to open those closed doors before me. After my ordination to priesthood had been canceled because of my blindness, my dear Bishop Reilly had appealed all the way to Pope Paul VI directly for the indult that had opened the door to priestly service for me.

A good friend, Deacon Eduardo Dogue, was on a conference committee preparing for a large conference several years ago. As he and the other committee workers were going over the spreadsheets detailing all of the proposed conference expenses, my friend began to laugh. His chuckling became so obvious that the conference convener finally asked what he had discovered in his study of the proposed budget. He said he was amazed as he looked at all that they were proposing to spend for speakers' travel, honoraria, fees, etc., and he thought of a speaker he knew who had gone all over the world, charging absolutely nothing for his talks and programs, trusting that a free-will offering would cover all of his travel and other expenses. "Even his books and CDs have no price tags on them. He's still on the road to this day ..."

"Oh, you're talking about Father Pat," the conference convener interrupted. "But all he talks about is God's love, and we need more than that here."

It took my friend several years before he had the courage to tell me that my not being on that conference speakers' list was not just an oversight; it was deliberate ... At first, his revelation did hurt me deeply. But that night, as I brought that hurt to prayer, God's healing voice brought untold peace and even joy to my bruised soul: "Patrick," he said so clearly, "that conference convener was dead right, was he not? Is there anything else that you speak about besides my redeeming love? Is there anything else you *need* to speak about besides my love?" His simple, healing words brought such peace and joy to my heart that night and confirmed my whole vocation to speak God's redeeming, helping love to this broken, suffering world. Imagine if my friend had never laughingly thought of me and if that conference convener had never asked the reason for his laughter!

In 1977, on a retreat preparing for my ordination to the priesthood, my retreat director asked me, "If you could have whatever you wanted from God this week, what would you ask for?"

I wonder if he thought I might ask for the curing of my eyes, but I didn't. I asked God for a picture of himself that I could show to this whole suffering world. God must surely have chuckled as he prepared his answer to my simple prayer request: "Has Patrick forgotten that he's blind? If I give him a wallet photo, he's the only one who won't be able to see it!" So, in his most creative love, God answered my prayer with a wallet photo that I could hear: a song that has now made its way all over this broken, suffering world!

He loves me. He loves me.

He loves me as I am. Oh yes, he loves me.

Yes, he loved me yesterday,

and yes, he'll love me still tomorrow,

For he loves me just today the way I am!

He loves me. He loves me.

And all he asks is that I let him love me,

Let him love me as he chooses,

With no thoughts for wins or loses,

Let him love me as I am is all he asks!

He knows me. He knows me.

Better than I know myself. Oh yes, he knows me.

Who I was the other day

And who I will become tomorrow,

But he loves me just today the way I am!

He calls me. He calls me.

He calls me as I am to spread his love.

Knowing well who I have been,

Who I will be, who I am,

Yet he calls me just the same to spread his love!

He frees me. He frees me.

He frees me to say yes whenever he calls me.

Showing me his own compassion,

Love and care and understanding.

He frees me to say my yes when He calls me!

He loves me. He loves me.

He loves me as I am. Oh yes, he loves me!

Finding me wherever I am,

He gently guides me by the hand,

For he loves me as I am. Oh, he loves me!

For he loves me as I am. Oh, he loves me!

Imagine if my retreat director had never asked me what I wanted most from my retreat? In 1977 on that retreat, God gave me his song picture, his love for me! His Holiness Pope Paul VI granted my dear Bishop Daniel Reilly a special indult, a papal permission, that same year to ordain me a blind priest! It was so exciting as preparations for my ordination day got underway. Invitations were prepared and printed and addressed to the thousands who had longed for this day almost more than I had! Looking for a souvenir memorial card that could be given to all who would come proved an almost impossible task. I just couldn't find the right card. I looked and looked and looked ... Then, in prayer one night, he spoke loud and clear: "I gave you my picture! When are you going to use it?"

I was most humbly awestruck. The song picture was immediately printed and given away to all who attended my ordination to priesthood on October 7, 1978! Since that awesome day, hundreds of thousands (millions?) more have been printed and given away! That conference convener many years ago was indeed dead right: I have absolutely nothing else to speak about, nothing else to live for! In 1977, God gave me his picture, the song of his love for me. In 1979, he called me to pray for Mother Mary's help to see that picture more clearly every day! My life today is only to discover, with Mary's help, God's love for me brand-new today, and my only ministry today is to help others to want to see God's love for them! Imagine if all in our world today, all of us, began yearning and praying daily for help to see God's love for us brand-new today. What a different world would be ours!

11 GOD'S DREAM, NOT MINE!

I chuckle as I look over my whole life and realize that at each step of life, I really had no idea where I was headed or why I was going there. I thought I knew. I wanted to be a priest. When I was told that was impossible, I settled on becoming a religious Brother. God had done so much for me in saving my life from meningitis; I wanted to now do for him in return. Closed doors were just obstacles to be overcome.

"Pawtrick, I think we're going to make a pretty good monk out of you!" I was so excited when I heard those words from my director at the Brothers' Prep High School in the fall of 1960. He teased me about being a French kid with an Irish name and so would pronounce it with a French twist.

By then, the Brothers knew all about my legal blindness, and they had decided to give me a chance anyway. With that major hurdle surmounted, I was now sure that I was where I could really do a lot for the good Lord, who had done so much for me.

I became a postulant with the Brothers in February 1963, graduated from the Brothers' Prep School in June, and officially became Brother Pat on August 22, 1963! A year later, I made my first vows as Brother Pat and then left for Walsh College—the Brothers' university in Canton, Ohio—to begin my studies for becoming a teaching Brother! I was excited. All was happening right on schedule. I was certain that I was where God wanted me, where I could do the most for him, who had done so much for me.

My first assignment as Brother Pat was at the Brothers' Denis Hall Jr. High School, a residential school in Alfred, Maine. The boarding school had no library, and so, in addition to teaching and doing secretarial work, I set to work setting up our first library for the teachers and students. Life in Alfred was rich; it was exciting. I absolutely loved living, praying, and working with my Brothers! Each day made me more sure I was where God wanted me.

After three years at the boarding school, I was awarded a federal grant to pursue master's degree studies at the Catholic University of America in Washington, D.C., to become the boarding school's first full-time librarian. I made my final vows as Brother Pat on August 22, 1969, and then left for my full year of studies in Washington. I was happy. I could see myself spending my whole life helping kids there at the boarding school. My own teachers back home had helped me so much. What a way I now had to give back what I had received!

When I left for the university in September 1969, my goal was clear. Because of my vision problem, reading one letter at a time, I was encouraged by the library school staff to take two or even three years to get through the degree program. I insisted on going through the program in one year, knowing that the boarding school needed a librarian. I was sure I knew God's plan for me to do his work.

I was at Catholic University only a few weeks, however, when everything turned upside down for my life. In a class discussion, I heard about "talking books" one evening. I had been reading letter-by-letter for seventeen years and had never heard about "talking books." A state counselor for the blind used to visit me in northern Maine once a year, and he had never mentioned the availability of talking books to help me in my studies. I read more with talking books that year than I had been able to reading in the seventeen years before it! With the help of recordings, I did indeed complete my master's degree studies in that one year! But I never returned to the boarding school …

What does it mean to be a Brother?" Robert S. Bray asked me one afternoon on one of my now regular visits to the Division for the Blind and Physically Handicapped of the Library of Congress. He was the chief of the division and had heard about this blind Brother who had just discovered the free services he could have used for seventeen years. He told me pleadingly that I was one of about ten million in the US who could be using talking books but knew nothing about them. He pleaded with me to get into the work and find those others like myself. With his help, the Brothers gave me permission to try the work as a Brother for a year ...

Life was suddenly moving so fast. My plans had been so clear, so definite: This is what I would do for God and his people. Suddenly, however, he seemed to be telling me what he wanted to do for me—and for his people *with* me! "You know why you were hired," Charlotte Harrison said as I reported for duty in September 1970. "You weren't hired to be a librarian behind a desk. You were hired to get out there and find the handicapped who know nothing about our services." And so this small-town boy from northern Maine, with street maps and subway maps of the city of New York, set to work finding the handicapped and helping them to find the city's accessible library services.

I loved New York! With all of its buses and trains and taxies and subways, I could go wherever and whenever to find my people and help them find our services. Like in the Brothers' boarding school, now here in New York I was sure I had found my work for God and his people. What an honor it was to be helping others like myself! I loved it!

"The Brothers taught you a lot about what it means to be a Brother," my superior told me on one of his visits to New York, "but the handicapped you are serving have made you their brother!"

I began my work by getting on the phone: calling hospitals, nursing homes, schools, parishes, churches, etc. and telling whomever about our library's services for those who couldn't handle regular print. My first four calls resulted in four invitations to come out and speak at staff meetings, etc. Within weeks, I was no longer calling them, they were calling me, and my calendar quickly filled itself in. Talks in the city soon led to requests for talks outside the city. Talks about talking books led to talks about suffering … My work was growing without my even seeing it. When the city's library finally said no to outreach talks beyond its jurisdiction, my superior with the Brothers challenged me to leave the city's employment and work for God, free to go wherever and whenever I was called! Just when I thought I finally knew what I could best do for God in return for all he had done for me, everything suddenly changed. Or did it really change at all?

My freelance work ultimately brought me to the diocese of Norwich, the Ministry of His Able People, Bishop Reilly, Pope Paul VI, and the priesthood! Wow! As a child twenty years earlier, I had been told that my dream of serving God as a priest was impossible. With Pope Paul's special permission, I realized that perhaps that childhood dream was not mine but God's! And after our "year of hell," when Bishop Reilly dissolved the entire ministry in 1980 and had us start all over again as a ministry *of* the handicapped instead of a ministry *for* the handicapped, then I knew that not only the dream but even the ministry was not mine, but his! God hadn't made me blind but had incredibly redeemed my blind life. Our newly refounded ministry was simply to bring that same message of God's life-redeeming love to others just like myself.

In the summer of 1979, several months after being called to ask our Mother Mary each morning to help me to see God's love for me today, I received a request from St. Michael's parish in Sunbury, Pennsylvania, to preach a retreat on God's love in our broken lives to the whole parish. I had preached many such retreats already, but all of them had been for groups of disabled retreatants. This would be my first opportunity to preach the message of God's life-redeeming love to a whole parish. Wow!

God is so patient in calling us, in leading us his way. Each time I thought I knew his plan for my broken life, he showed me how right I was—and how wrong I was! Yes, he has indeed called me to this point on my life's journey, but no, this isn't the complete journey. This is truly but one more step on his called journey! I had thought my calling was to the library for the handicapped of New York, and through Charlotte Harrison, he made it clear that my calling went far outside the walls of that library! I was so happy and fulfilled, doing his work there in New York City, and then he called me from New York to Norwich, Connecticut. Ah! Now working for the Church instead of for the city, I was home, where I was sure he wanted me! Then requests from beyond the diocese, and my Bishop's words told me that I still didn't know the extent of God's calling in my broken life: "Patrick, I've ordained you for your work, not to take you from it! Your parish is the entire world! Get out and find the broken like yourself and help them to find God's love for them as you've found it!"

His words were so much like the command of Charlotte Harrison when my work in New York had first begun: "You know why you were hired … Get out and find the handicapped like yourself and help them to find our services!" With the Sunbury, Pennsylvania, request, I came to see that God's calling seemed not only to go far beyond library walls or geographical borders but also beyond definitions of brokenness. "All of my people are handicapped," the Sunbury pastor had said. "Some of them know it, and others don't." Wow! Bit by bit, I was learning that this really wasn't my work, my dream, my ministry. Someone else really was in charge.

Through the clergy grapevine, the Sunbury parish mission led to a similar mission in Glastonbury, Connecticut. News of those two brought requests from Ontario, Canada, and from the Rosebud Indian Reservation in South Dakota … In 1991, with the mission requests streaming in constantly, I was freed full-time for that on-the-road work. Today, over

1,300 parish missions have brought me all over the English-speaking world, and the requests are still streaming in.

It frightens me when I hear people say, "I don't have to pray for help to see God's love for me today, Father. I know his love already." As a blind child saved from meningitis, I thought I knew God's love. Accepted by the Brothers, I was sure I knew God's love. On October 7, 1978, as my dear Bishop Daniel P. Reilly laid his ordaining hands on my head, God's love for me was so evident. At Easter 1979, with a peace that my ministry troubles couldn't disturb, I was overwhelmed with the awareness of God's love for me! That Easter, however, I had no idea the gifts of love that God had yet waiting for me on my life's journey! Yes, I would have said that I really knew his love. In reality, I realize now that I didn't even have a clue!!! Look at what his love has done with my life since that Easter! It makes me excited as I now look at tomorrow ... Mary, help me to see God's love for me today!

12 GOD'S DOOR OPENERS

As I continue to pray each morning after three dozen years now for Mother Mary's help to see God's love for me today, most of the time I seem to be praying in front of yet more closed doors. I'm asking Mary to help me see her son fulfilling that promise he had given me at that prayer meeting in June 1972: "Behold, I will set a door open before you which none will shut again" (Rev. 3:18).

As I look back at my life, I am amazed at the number of slammed-shut doors there have been on my life's journey. Our family doctor quit my case, telling my folks they were fools to hope for my life. As I left the hospital almost five months later, they were told I'd never walk again. They were told that because of my blindness, I couldn't go to school at home, I couldn't serve Mass in our parish church, I couldn't become a priest ... And, with an attack of sciatica four years ago and the bleeding that came from its medication, I was told I wouldn't live anymore …

Those are but a few of the closed doors that have pockmarked my life's road since I was nine. Praying for Mother Mary's help to see God's love for me today has helped me to see those closed doors through her eyes! For every single closed door, it's almost incredible, but God has provided a door opener for me exactly as he promised: "Behold, I will set a door open before you which none will ever shut again!"

Dr. Warren was hired by the hospital to replace our quitting family doctor. Studying my case and reading about the new antibiotics that were just hitting the medical market, he decided to "try" … After almost three months in a coma, life's door was cracked open for me! After five months in the hospital, that door was opened wide as I was discharged and sent home for Christmas! I had to be carried home from the hospital because I couldn't walk. Physical therapy hardly existed in medicine in those days, but God turned my own brothers and sisters into the best of therapists for me. Holding me up by the shoulders, they'd escort me up and down the hallway at home. "We won't let you fall," they'd assure me as they encouraged me to take one, then two, then three steps on my own! And in a month and a half, those budding physical therapists had opened the door to walking for me …

The state of Maine sent us to eye specialists all over the area to see if anything could be done for my destroyed vision, but all the experts handed down the same verdict: "Send him to a school for the blind." I wanted so much to be able to go off to school with my brothers and sisters. But I was told that door was closed. I would have to go to school about 500 miles from home. That seemed like the end of the world to me.

Then, my dear sister Lorraine talked to a teacher she knew and loved at our local school. Telling her about my blindness, Lorraine told her how sad it was that at ten years old, I would have to go away to school ... Mrs. McGill, that dear angel teacher, asked the town, "Why should this kid go to school 500 miles from home when we can teach him right here at home?" Long before mainstreaming of the handicapped was ever thought of educationally, she opened yet another closed door for me!

And what doors, indeed, she opened for me that year! She not only caught me up with my fellow students after more than a year out of school, but she gave me gifts that year that would open other doors in my years ahead. Seeing that my destroyed vision was pinpoint, she taught me to type, explaining that the typewriter would tell me at the end of a line and would even find the next line for me! She taught me to memorize "important stuff" as I read along letter-by-letter. "You won't need to reread over and over again," she explained ... Wow! What an angel!

Mrs. McGill had no idea the doors her taught skills would eventually open for me! Memorizing was especially fantastic in our parish religion classes on Saturday mornings.

We used the *Baltimore Catechism*, a book of questions and answers on our Catholic faith. Each year, we students were expected to learn a few more chapters. In my fifth grade year, I memorized the entire catechism, cover to cover. In the contest at the end of the year, competing with all students in grades first through eighth, I came away the winner! I went over to the young priest in our parish, Fr. Richard Poulin, after the contest to have my prize blessed. After blessing the beautiful statue of Our Lady that I had won, he surprised me fantastically with his door-opening question: "How come you aren't an altar server?"

"I'm blind," I stammered in utter surprise.

"If you can memorize the whole catechism," he answered, "you can learn to serve at Mass! I will teach you."

I don't know if that young priest ever knew the hope he enkindled in a blind child's heart that day! I served Mass every morning from then onward. On my way to school, I would stop at church, serve the morning Mass for the parish, and then go on my way. As those wonderful years passed by, I found myself thinking more and more about the next closed doors on my path ...

"What will I have to do to become a priest?" I asked our pastor one morning after Mass. He cried as he told me that he had already checked with the seminary, and they had assured him that my blindness was a real door closer there. A blind priest might spill the chalice, drop the communion hosts, and of course, couldn't read the Latin … I cried when I left him that day … Up to then in my life, I saw people as the real door closers and door openers in life. If I could only get them to give me a chance, I was sure I could succeed just fine. Now I began to see blindness itself as the real door closer of my life. Even if they would give me a chance, there were actually things I could not do because I was blind …

When Robert S. Bray of the Library of Congress first challenged me to get into the talking books work in 1970, he said something that truly puzzled me: "With your blindness, you're actually one of them. They'll listen to you." He was truly the first who had ever spoken of my being blind as an asset. It intrigued me. Then, a short time after actually starting my talking books work at the New York Public Library, one of my bosses called and said she was sending Mary Engels from the *New York Daily News* down for an interview. When I objected, saying I really didn't want the publicity, she retorted immediately that my story in the paper would most certainly help them find others like myself who knew nothing about the talking books! And she was right. My story in the *Daily News* that weekend actually found 165 new talking books users by itself!

Several years later, long after I had moved to the diocese of Norwich and long after I had been ordained as a blind priest, I was asked to visit a federal prison. The warden, who had been at one of my parish missions on God's love in our broken lives, had explained that they had a young prisoner in solitary confinement who was a danger to himself and to everyone else. No one could get through to the young man. Could I possibly come and talk with him?

At first, the prisoner just clammed up, saying he was sure I was just like everyone else who had tried to help him. I listened to his jabbering for a while and then said, "Would you shut up for one minute!" His fists came out of his pockets, clenched for the attack. But before his fists could attack, I attacked with words: "Do you want to get out from behind these bars? Change your attitude!" Then I went on to say that some of us live behind bars from which we can't escape. He snarled at that point: "What do you know about living behind bars?" I hadn't been able to bring my white cane, etc. into the prison, so I simply said, "When I can't recognize my own mother on the sidewalk ... When I get a handwritten note and can't read it ... When I get a call for help and can't go because I can't drive a car ... I know a bit what it's like to live behind bars."

Years later, I can still hear his next words in my ears: "You got trouble with your eyes, Reverend?"

After hearing that I was blind, the prisoner, crying profusely, sat right down on the floor of his cell, and I sat right down with him. After an hour and a half or so, I left the prison, thanking God for what he had done with my blindness that day. He hadn't made me blind, but he had made my very blindness the door opener to that young prisoner's heart! Wow!

Several months after my prison visit, I spoke to a school assembly: 600 students and faculty gathered to hear about God's love in our broken lives. I pray only that those students and faculty remember only a tiny bit of what I said that day as well as I remember the student's thank you at the end: "Father Pat, we, the students and faculty of Holy Cross High School, want to thank you sincerely today for being blind!" Wow!

13 BLINDNESS, MY GREATEST TEACHER

The greatest down closer of my life has become truly my greatest door opener for others! Wow! Only God! In December 2012, while preaching a mission in Ocala, Florida, I awoke one night with screeching pain from my right hip to the very tips of my toes. No matter what I did during the next days of the mission, no matter what pills I took, the pain got steadily worse. Standing, sitting, lying down—nothing changed the pain. Finally, after the mission, I went to the local hospital, where my pain was diagnosed as sciatica! A couple of shots and a couple of prescriptions for pain meds took care of everything. I hugged the doctor as I left the hospital pain free.

Lynn and Rich Sbardella of Stafford Springs, Connecticut, had worked as volunteers for me for twenty years, taking care of all of the ministry's secretarial and banking work. Leaving the Florida hospital, I decided to go to their home in Connecticut to recuperate. But my strength just wouldn't come back. I seemed to be getting weaker with each passing day. By the fourth day, I was pain free still, but I was so weak that I could hardly stand up unassisted. My secretary drove me to the local hospital, which immediately transferred me to a larger hospital in Hartford. I was bleeding internally. The medication that so wondrously stopped my sciatica pain had burned three holes in my stomach! After several weeks of fruitless efforts to stop the bleeding, I was getting weaker and weaker.

Missions were canceled … My family was called … I was in the hospital almost a month before they finally stopped the bleeding. I had lost more than forty pounds and could no longer stand up, let alone walk. When the bleeding was finally stopped, the hospital decided it was time for a nursing home. I remember those hospital days so vividly. One test after another, more rooms than I could count … But strangely, more peace than I could have ever imagined I would have. The ministry was at a stand-still. My dear mission scheduler, Jim Oscar, was canceling missions one week at a time. My dear webmaster, Jeanne Filek, was keeping all inquirers up to date with weekly emails. And my secretary, Lynn, kept everybody posted by phone. And I lay in my hospital bed at peace.

One night, lying in my hospital bed, I suddenly saw the most beautiful scene on the wall at the foot of my bed: My own body was lying there, with thousands of hands and arms holding me up from head to toe! As I gazed in wonder at the scene, I asked in prayer whose many hands and arms were holding me up. "Those are all the ones who never stop praying for you these days. Their prayers have helped you to find peace here no matter what" was the simple answer I got! No wonder I was in such peace no matter what. Wow!

My only prayer in that hospital each day, after asking our Blessed Mother Mary to help me to see God's love for me today, was so simply "Lord, do with this what you've done with my blindness, and I'll be a truly happy camper!" I had never prayed for my blindness to go away, and now I prayed only that God would redeem my sciatica and my bleeding as he had so dearly redeemed my blindness! I went through more tests and scans than I could count and was transferred to at least half a dozen different rooms in the hospital in my almost one month there. My only prayer was the constant "Lord, help me to serve you from all these hospital beds as you've helped me to spread your love from the pulpit of my blindness!" God's redeeming love with my blindness has become the greatest teacher of my life!

After almost a month in that hospital, the real source of my bleeding was finally discovered: The holes that had been burned in my stomach were now well scarred over but were actually still bleeding from beneath the scars … In a final surgery, clamps were inserted, and the bleeding stopped. I had now lost more than forty pounds, however, and was unable to stand erect, let alone walk …

My sister, Patricia, who had come all the way from San Antonio, Texas, for what was realistically expected to be my funeral, now heard the hospital staff talking about a nursing home transfer. "He's not going to a nursing home," she said.

"Where's he going? He can't stay here," the attending doctor responded.

"He's coming home with me," she said.

Despite assurances that I wouldn't survive the flights, she helped me discharge myself, and with wheelchair helpers, I did indeed make it from Hartford to Dallas and from Dallas to San Antonio!

God bless my dear sister and brother-in-law, Patricia and Deacon Jerome Kozar. I first met Jerry on their wedding day! That was my first family visit home from the Brothers. Since then, he's become closer to me than any of all my siblings. Now, almost fifty years later, he and my sister made their San Antonio home my home and connected me with all the services I needed. They arranged with a doctor in the parish, Dr. Matthew Gibbs, to take charge medically, and he set me up with all the medical care I needed.

After three weeks in bed, my sister asked one morning, "Would you like to try a walker?" I trusted her totally. With her help, I was soon out of bed and on my feet again. After a few weeks with that borrowed walker, my brother-in-law brought me to a medical supply place, and I came home with my "Cadillac" of walkers! That walker has traveled thousands of miles with me now, still spreading the good news of God's love for his broken people.

When I left the hospital in Connecticut, it was presumed I'd never get back on the road again—my work was done. With the encouragement and blessings of my dearest sister and brother-in-law, my Norwich Bishop Cote, and finally, my dear San Antonio Archbishop Gustavo, San Antonio became home for me! And then I began to get better!

"Are you ever going to get back to your mission work?" a priest from western Canada asked one day on the phone.

"Father," I responded, "I'm walking with a walker."

"Well, bring the walker," he responded immediately. "All we want is your voice!"

And so I preached to his mission and three other missions with my walker that year, and now dozens more, as before! And my dear walker travels all over with me! A dear friend, Jay Petronio from Providence, Rhode Island, affectionately named my walker "Jesus 1." "If the President travels with Air Force 1," he said, "you travel just as much with Jesus 1!"

14 FREE TO HELP OTHERS

I have had the most wonderful team of doctors and other medical personnel here in San Antonio these past five years. They're constantly blessing me, and my body hasn't exactly made it easy for them. About a year ago, I broke out in a rash all over my body. My physical strength began to wane again. Several doctors worked hand in hand, trying to relieve the rash and find its cause. All efforts seemed fruitless. For years and years now, I've been on blood pressure medications, and so it was finally assumed that one of these medications must be the culprit. Thus began the long and tedious task of testing my meds one by one. And as the meds were manipulated, so was my blood pressure. Meanwhile, the rash got no better and my strength never returned.

In the summer of 2017, with my missions being canceled and others held off from being scheduled at all, uncertain as to whether or not I'd ever be able to get back to a full schedule of missions, I was given permission to formally retire as a priest. "Ave Maria Place," which had been my ministry's headquarters since the 1970s, was now formally closed. I said goodbye to my secretary and her husband, who had worked with me since the early 1990s ... I was officially retired as of October 1, 2017. A week later, my rash *disappeared!* Again I was back in my dear doctors' offices. They were as baffled as I was, finally attributing the rash, etc. to stress ...

My kidney specialist during all this time had the fantastic inspiration to check out the artery from my kidney to my heart. "If it's constrained," he said, "we can do balloon therapy to open it up and, hopefully, thereby bring your blood pressure readings closer to normal and thereby eliminate many of these medications that you're now on." With only one kidney, I've been plagued with high blood pressure for close to fifty years now. I was excited as he scheduled me for the test, but utterly shocked when I was given the results of the test. While looking at my one kidney and its artery, my fantastic doctor had discovered a mass growing on the end of the kidney. It was cancer ... How appropriate it was, I thought, that I was now retired.

The news of the cancer cast me down for a short time that day ... Then, in prayer that night, God spoke: "Patrick," he said, "I redeemed your meningitis because you gave it to me. I redeemed your blindness because you gave it to me ... I can't redeem this cancer if you don't give it to me."

My prayer was suddenly flooded with tears that night, but they were tears of joy and relief. "It's all yours," I said to my most loving redeemer that night. "I don't ask you to take away this cancer but only to do with it as you've so lovingly done with my blindness. Use it—please, please, please—to do good for others!"

Cancer, the "big C," is truly one of the most feared medical diagnoses in our world today. I suddenly got so excited that night as I contemplated yet another avenue I now had for bringing peace and hope to my fellow suffering people. I was one of them in yet another way!

From that moment onward, I have been *free*. I have had peace—peace that even cancer could not destroy! I had surgery on November 21, two days before Thanksgiving, and a couple days later was discharged to join my dear sister and brother-in-law and my nephew, Andy, at home for a fantastic Thanksgiving dinner! Three weeks later, with the awesome blessing of my kidney specialist, I flew to Fort Meyers, Florida, to St. Cecelia's parish for a Christmas mission on God's redeeming love in our broken lives!

I had no chemo, no radiation … The surgeon simply went in with a needle, guided by robots, and microwaved the tumor! Several months of home health care and physical therapy graduated me once again. Wow! And now, in the summer of 2018, I've just finished preaching a half dozen more parish missions on God's love in our broken lives in Florida, New York, New England, and here in San Antonio!

Only a God of love! I wonder now how he will turn even my cancer into gift, as he has all the other sufferings of my broken life! He truly does redeem my life from destruction ... and he's very evidently not done yet! Because of his redeeming love, I am truly free at last: free from discouragement, free from fear, free from anger, free from sadness ... *Free at last!*

Yes, the God who doesn't give us our sufferings most assuredly does redeem our broken lives from destruction! He gives us hope, no matter what sufferings this world dumps upon us. I pray every morning still, after thirty-nine years, for the help of his dearest Mother Mary to see his redeeming love for me in my sufferings today, and I pray each evening in true thanksgiving for the gift he has made of my suffering life today. God's redeeming love has spoken so often, so loudly, no matter what sufferings: "I love you, Patrick!"

Mary, my mother, help me to see God's love for me today! Mary, gift of your son's love for me, I love and cherish you! Giver of your son's love to me, I love and cherish you! Sight for my blind eyes, I love and cherish you! Way to my lonely heart's peace, I love and cherish you! Vision of God's love for me, I love and cherish you dearly.

15 I'M NOT ALONE ANYMORE!

When people come to see me in the midst of their own sufferings, I beg them to please pray every morning for our Mother Mary's help to see God's love for them today. Most respond immediately that they already know God loves them … They're just like me, I realize today. For years, I was sure I knew God's love for me. I had heard and felt his "I love you" more times than I could ever count! I knew that he loved me … but I realize now that I didn't know his love for me at all. Praying for Mary's help to see his love for me today opens my blind eyes to really see his love for me today like I've never dreamed of seeing it before.

The most astounding vision of God's love for me that's come with that daily prayer is the realization that I'm really not alone anymore. In fact, I've never really been alone! His love has been with me through all of my seventy-four years now. I always saw God's helping hand in my life growing up. I have no memories of the first nine years of my life; the meningitis took those memories away. But I remember vividly coming home from the hospital on December 22, 1953, and all the many other milestones thereafter: learning to walk, going back to my hometown school, learning to type and to memorize, entering the Brothers … I have countless vivid memories of God's miracles in my life. Yes, I knew for sure that God loved me. But I didn't really know his love for me …

As I've prayed day after day, week after week, month after month, year after year for thirty-nine-plus years now for Mary's help to see God's love for me today, I'm coming now to see God's love for me more than in what he does for me … He's *with* me no matter what!

In the spring of 1988, I was privileged to be able to make the thirty-day retreat of St. Ignatius of Loyola to celebrate my first ten years of priesthood and my twenty-five years of religious life. Yes, it's a silent retreat, and yes, I actually kept silent for those thirty days! Fifty-seven of us retreatants from all over the world gathered at the Jesuit retreat house in Guelph, Ontario, Canada, for the retreat experience. Each of us was assigned a retreat director who guided us individually through our thirty days of renewal. May I never forget that life-changing night in the middle of my retreat … My director assigned the scriptural Christmas story as my meditation for that night. I was instructed to read the passage several times and then to let my memory, my imagination, and all of my senses plunge me into the story. What an experience of God's love exploded for me right there in my retreat house room! Suddenly, I found myself right there in Bethlehem's cave. It was dark, and so I was afraid of making a disturbance by tripping over a sheep, a camel, one of the shepherds, or a root or rock in the floor of the cave. I carefully found my way to the very back of the cave and sat down right on the earthen floor with my back up against the cave's stone wall. I didn't make a sound. As my eyes slowly adjusted to the dim light, I found myself surveying the scene before me, and finally, my blind eyes landed on *them!* I was sure it was Mary and Joseph. They were sitting against the cave's opposite wall, with all the shepherds, sheep, the wisemen, and their retinue between me and them. I couldn't make out the child, but I was sure he was right there between Mary and Joseph.

I remember the scene so well. It was vivid. I could feel the cool air, the dampness of the earthen floor, and the cold rocks against my back. In the stillness, I could actually hear the breathing of the shepherds, the wisemen, and their animals. It was awesome. And then I saw movement. Joseph was leaning over toward Mary. Their heads seemed to be turned toward me? They were talking, but I couldn't hear their words. Oh, how I wanted them to be looking at me!

Then, with my pinpoint vision, I watched as Joseph got to his feet and began to walk across the cave, right toward me! My heart was beating out of my chest as he leaned over, touched my shoulder, and said, "Mary wants to know if you'd like to hold the child." I don't remember saying anything. He helped me to my feet and ever so carefully guided me across the room, around this sheep, that camel, this shepherd, that wiseman … over this root and carefully around this rock … Finally, we were right next to Mary. She was holding the infant in her arms. Ever so gently, Joseph took the child from Mary's arms and placed him in my most unworthy embrace … I don't know how long I held the child. Holding his tiny body against my heart, I remember just rocking back and forth, swooning so gently, even humming a lullaby. Tears of unbelievable joy coursed down my cheeks, and I made no effort to take them away.

After a long time, Joseph gently took the child from my arms and placed him back in his mother's lap. I sat there in silence for a long time, pondering what had just happened. Finally, I looked into Mary's eyes and asked, "Why did you invite me to hold the child? Why not one of the shepherds or wisemen?"

Then Mary answered with words I've never forgotten in these thirty years! "You looked so alone over there," Mary spoke so gently to me, " and my son came for those who are alone, you know."

Wow! In that one sentence, Mary summarized all of salvation for me: "You looked so alone over there, and my son came for those who are alone, you know." He came for me in my aloneness ...

The contemplation ended, but my prayer did not. I found myself now walking down the walkways of my life. And for most of that walking, I was indeed alone. Physically, I had been far from alone growing up. My parents, brothers and sisters, aunts and uncles, cousins, teachers, etc. just couldn't do enough for me. My coming home from the hospital that December in 1953 had made Christmas for them. They had been more excited than I was! But in so many ways, I was alone ... or I thought I was alone. With my blindness, those growing-up years I always felt alone, different. I had to find other ways to do things that others seemed to do so easily. Many of life's normal open doors were closed to me.

"You looked so alone over there, and my son came for those who are alone, you know." Wow! When my dear Bishop Reilly gave me permission to make that thirty-day anniversary retreat, I really had no idea the gift he was giving me. Mary's words in that Christmas contemplation truly unlocked the door to life's chamber of peace for me. With her dear words, I found myself again walking down the pathways of my life, but I wasn't alone on that walk this time. I saw that Jesus was right there walking with me! Wow!

In early August 2018, my dear sister Patricia got a
phone call asking if I might be available to come and
celebrate a Mass for them at the Villa de San Antonio. My
sister has taken care of all my scheduling since I moved to
San Antonio in 2013, but she's always so careful to get my
okay for appointments. This appointment left me curious,
however. What was this Villa de San Antonio, I wondered?

Beverly, the caller, invited me and my sister and brother-
in-law to come and see—to come for lunch one day. We
went, and the rest is history! I don't remember much about
the wonderful tour we had that day, only that the chapel
where I would celebrate Mass for the residents and visitors
of the villa had absolutely no steps and no rugs for me to
trip over! Our tour ended with a fantastic lunch in the
villa's restaurant dining room. Near the end of our meal, I
exclaimed, to the shock of my sister, "I'd love to live here!"
I had no idea when I had agreed to come and check out the
place for my possibly coming to celebrate Mass that I was
actually checking out my future home!

My superior with the Brothers had said to me years
earlier, "We Brothers taught you much about being a
Brother, but those you serve now have actually made
you their brother." And now, it was the same. I had lived
with my dear sister and brother-in-law and my nephew
and their dear three dogs for almost six years. They had
most assuredly saved my life, I am sure! We were family,
I thought, forever … But now I was truly being called to

let the residents and staff of the Villa de San Antonio be my brothers and sisters. Brother Francis had said so dearly to me one evening, "Brother Pat, you never left the Brothers at all. You went to the handicapped and the priesthood as our Brother Pat! You're still very much a Brother with us." And now I was called—not to leave my dear San Antonio family but to bring the life my family had saved for me to my brothers and sisters who needed me at the Villa de San Antonio. Wow!

As this book finally goes to press, I've now been a resident at the Villa de San Antonio for a couple of weeks. I join many of the residents for the Chaplet of Divine Mercy and the Rosary each afternoon at three o'clock, at daily Mass, at meals, and at many other activities. I celebrate the Mass for my fellow residents each Sunday morning in that fantastic chapel! And, thanks to fantastic volunteers, I'm still available to help out at St. Anthony Claret and other parishes, and my on-the-road missions are still scheduling! What excites me most about this move in my life is that it really wasn't my move! Had that call from Beverly never come in, I would have never thought of moving. I was perfectly happy living with my dear family. It's like God slapped me upside the head and said, "Okay, you've recuperated long enough. It's time to get back to the work for which I've called you!"

I'm not alone anymore! Actually, I've never really been alone. With my blind eyes focused on myself, I so often presumed that I was all alone. In his walk with me down the pathways of my life, Jesus showed me so gently but so firmly that he's been with me through it all. And he's still with me today, even in these so-called retirement years! My life, my ministry isn't over yet. "It ain't over till I hear him singing, and I don't even hear him warming up yet!" His loving presence brings me peace today no matter what, no matter when, no matter where! Wow! Fantastic!

"Litany of Love"

Lord, have mercy!

> *Christ, have mercy!*

Lord, have mercy on us.

> *Christ, hear us!*

Christ, graciously hear us!

God the Father of Heaven, Lord, You love us!

> *God the Son, Redeemer of the world, Lord, You love us!*

God the Holy Spirit, Lord, You love us!

> *Holy Trinity, One God, Lord, You love us!*

In all of creation, Lord, You love us!

In all of salvation, Lord, You love us!

In all of holiness, Lord, You love us!

In all of redemption, Lord, You love us!

In Your incarnation, Lord, You love us!

In Your obedience to Your Father, Lord, You love us!

In Your obedience to Mary and Joseph, Lord, You love us!

In Your preaching and healing, Lord, You love us!

In Your feeding and forgiving, Lord, You love us!

In all Your sufferings, Lord, You love us!

In Your crucifixion, Lord, You love us!

In Your death and burial, Lord, You love us!

In Your rising from the dead, Lord, You love us!

In Your ascension to Your Father, Lord, You love us!

In Your gift of the Holy Spirit, Lord, You love us!

In Your body and blood, Lord, You love us *dearly*!

In the gift of Your love for us, Lord, You love us *dearly*!

In all our peace, Lord, You love us!

In all our joys, Lord, You love us!

In all our trials, Lord, You love us!

In all our pains, Lord, You love us!

In all our struggles, Lord, You love us!

In all our questions, Lord, You love us!

In all our answers, Lord, You love us!

In all our unknowing, Lord, You love us!

In all our searching, Lord, You love us!

In all our finding, Lord, You love us!

In all our family, Lord, You love us!

In all our friends, Lord, You love us!

In all our homes, Lord, You love us!

In all our love, Lord, You love us!

In all our tears, Lord, You love us!

In all our aloneness, Lord, You love us!

In all our brokenness, Lord, You love us!

In all our sinfulness, Lord, You love us!

In all our forgiveness, Lord, You love us!

In all our forgivingness, Lord, You love us!

In all we love, Lord, You love us!

In all who love us, Lord, You love us!

In all our work, Lord, You love us!

In all our play, Lord, You love us!

In all our prayer, Lord, You love us!

In all our sharing, Lord, You love us!

In all our silence, Lord, You love us!

In all our dreams, Lord, You love us!

In all our fears, Lord, You love us!

In all our hopes, Lord, You love us!

In all our disappointments, Lord, You love us!

In all our helpers, Lord, You love us!

In all those we help, Lord, You love us!

In all our yesterdays, Lord, You love us!

In all our tomorrows, Lord, You love us!

In our right now, Lord, You love us dearly!

In all Your angels, Lord, You love us!

In all Your saints, Lord, You love us!

In our Blessed Mother Mary, Lord, You love us dearly!

Lamb of God, Who takes away all the sins of the world, Lord, You love us!

Lamb of God, Who takes away all the sins of the world, Lord, You love us!

Lamb of God, Who takes away all the sins of the world, Lord, You love us dearly!

Lord, You love us dearly!

May we love You more and more every moment of life that's ours! May our every thought, wish, word, action, breath, and heartbeat from this moment of life onward be simply and truly a "Lord, You love us!" May all that's us and all that's ours (*all that's us and all that's ours*) exist only to say, to sing, to proclaim, to live, "Lord, You love us dearly!" We ask this special Grace of an all-loving heart in Your holy name, Jesus Christ, our Lord! Amen.

Romans 8:35–39 states:

> What will separate us from the love of Christ? Will anguish, or distress, or persecution, or famine, or nakedness, or peril, or the sword? As it is written:
>
> > "For your sake we are being slain all the day; we are looked upon as sheep to be slaughtered."
>
> No, in all these things we conquer overwhelmingly through him who loved us. For I am convinced that neither death, nor life, nor angels, nor principalities, nor present things, nor future things, nor powers,

nor height, nor depth, nor any other creature will be able to separate us from the love of God in Christ Jesus our Lord.

16 THE HOLY ROSARY, A GIFT FOR YOU

The dream of independence eventually sours into the nightmare of aloneness. Can I ever forget my first Christmas in my beloved New York? The library had graciously given me vacation time to spend the Christmas days with my family in Maine. I was so excited as I headed for LaGuardia Airport that December 1970 afternoon. It was a gorgeous suit-jacket-warm afternoon. Several had offered me help, but I had politely declined, proud as ever that I could make it on my own! And then I discovered at the airport that snow storms in Maine had stopped all air, train, and bus transportation into the state. I spent that Christmas alone. I had already many friends in New York, but you don't bother people on Christmas ...

"People who need people are the luckiest people in the world!" How gently and patiently Mary, the Mother of God and my dearest Mother, has schooled me these years into daring to need others' help in my life. With blindness, physical disabilities, and now hearing loss, too, my life is so rich because of all the heavenly and earthly helpers that grace it! There's never a day now that I don't pray earnestly, "Mary, help me to see God's love for me today!" And every day, every hour, every moment, I discover his love for me in the countless helpers he sends my way! Today, I give out rosaries at every parish mission I preach, begging people to pray as I have learned: "Mary, help me to see God's love for me today!" What a fantastic world we'd have if every single person prayed daily for Mary's help to see God's love for them today!

My dear brother Gerard Martin ("Gerry," as we called him) was truly the founder of our ministry's rosary-giving ministry. He begged rosaries from Legion of Mary groups, altar societies, and even individual rosary makers that he knew, so I would have rosaries to give away at every parish mission I preached! When his groups and volunteers died out, he learned to make rosaries himself! He would package the boxes of handmade rosaries and ship them off to every parish on my mission schedule. He continued making rosaries for my missions until his death in December 2011.

My dear brother Gerry not only started our rosary-giving ministry for my parish missions, but he also saw to it that his beautiful ministry would continue long after his death. He not only learned to make our needed rosaries, but he also taught others to make them for us as well! He got our dear mother Amanda to make her first one on Mother's Day one year, and her dear rosary work continued until her death in 1992! Gerry and Mom got our aunt Phoebe and uncle Ken to join their special ministry, and they, too, continued right up till their deaths! Then there was Marie Lasalle, who taught Gerry to make the chain rosaries and then joined his rosary-making ministry for our parish missions! And even when Gerry retired, he took his rosary-making supplies with him to his retirement home, where he got a fellow resident, Diane, to join his "retirement work!" She not only learned rosary-making from Gerry but also learned his Catholic faith from him! When Gerry died, all his rosary-making supplies were passed on to his special recruit!

In 1991, my dear Bishop Daniel Reilly made my on-the-road missions my full-time work. My full-time volunteer secretary, Lynn Sbardella, along with her family, joined the rosary-making brigade and took over the parish mission rosary-shipping work. Dear friends Stanley and Pat Antonovich from Belchertown, Massachusetts, took over the rosary-making-and-shipping work from Lynn and recruited many other volunteers to help them. Their volunteer helpers weren't locals only but included Bernie and Carol Sens from Oxford, Ohio, as well as Bill and

Donna Rechner, Bob and Helen Wise, and Beaver and Fran Schwarz all the way from Springfield, Illinois! The Illinois group recruited their own volunteers and started their own rosary-making group for our missions!

And then I moved to San Antonio, Texas! Maria Herrera, a parishioner in my new home parish, St. Anthony Mary Claret, just happened to have a rosary-making group in the parish. That group has now made *thousands* of rosaries for my parish missions! And now, as this dear Rosary book goes to press, Maria's group is making rosaries to be given with each published book! The rosary attached to this book is a gift to you from Maria's dear rosary-making group! Wow!

I grew up in a family that prayed the Rosary daily. During my 1953 illness that hospitalized me for five months, my family prayed the Rosary constantly for my recovery. In 1963, entering the Brothers of Christian Instruction, I embraced the way of the world and threw my Rosary away. In Lent of 1979, the good shepherd who goes out searching for his lost sheep brought me home to our Mother Mary and her rosary. When my parish missions got started that very year, it was only natural that God would get me to give to others what he had just given to me! As you pick up the rosary gift that comes with this book, I pray that it will become for you the life-saving gift it has truly become for me!

Hail Mary, full of grace,

the Lord is with you.

Blessed are you among women,

and blessed is the fruit of your womb, Jesus!

Holy Mary, Mother of God,

pray for us sinners,

now and at the hour of our death.

Amen.

Mary, mother of our savior, help us to see God's love for us today!

17 THANK YOU! THANK YOU! THANK YOU!

Thank you, thank you, thank you to all of this book's generous sponsors. I pray that I'm Not Alone Anymore! has blessed you as you read it, and I pray that it will bless countless more readers because of your sponsorship. May God bless you forever!

Fr. Pat

Aldaya, George and Michele, San Antonio, TX

For our family and especially our sons in the military

Ames, Richard and Diane, Weston, FL

In thanksgiving

Ambrosy, Donald, Glendale, AV

Don and Jan Ambrosy and family

Arcebielo, Tina, Weston, FL

In thanksgiving

Arcos, Mrs. Eva D., Hondo, TX

In memory of my husband, Simon S. Arcos Sr.

Ayinkamiye, Immaculee, Saco, ME

In thanksgiving

Aloys et Immaculee et leurs enfants

In thanksgiving

Azzarone, Anna, Cranston, RI

My guardian-angel daughters, Ann Marie and Maria

Bagnowski, Audrey Ann, Rockwood, MI

In thanksgiving for God's lifelong blessings, love, care, and protection

Bakita, John and Patricia, The Villages, FL

In thanksgiving

Barker, Elaine A., Haverhill, MA

For special intention

Benson, Andra and Chuck, Sansing, NY

Prayers for my husband's and son's health and freedom from pain

Bergkamp, Dennis and Kathy, San Antonio, TX

In thanksgiving

Bertucci, Rich and Roni, Pompano Beach, FL

In loving memory of our parents, Raymond and Carmen Quintanilla

Biggs, Lorraine, Anaconda, MT

In thanksgiving

Birchall, Vivian J., Cobble Hill, BC, CANADA

Jesus, I trust in you!

Blanchette, Blanche, Fort Kent, ME

To my husband, Real

Bochniewicz, Anne, West Hartford, CT

In thanksgiving

Bosse, Paul E., Garden Grove, CA

In thanksgiving

Bourassa, Raymond, Brandon, MB, CANADA

May Jesus love you, Fr. Pat

Brady, Raymond and Alice, N. Providence, RI

In thanksgiving

Braun, Christopher and Diane, Hayesville, NC

For the holy souls in Purgatory

Bivau, Joanne, Hamilton, ONT, CANADA

Brown, Mrs. Delma, Sault Ste. Marie, ONT, CANADA

John Brown

Brown, Doug and Julia, Davie, FL

Praise and thanksgiving for all God's blessings!

Brown, James H., Blairsville, GA

In memory of my mother, Betty A. Brown

Brunsman, Deacon Bill and Betty, Hamilton, OH

In thanksgiving

Buechel, Richard and Sharon, Dryden, NY

In thanksgiving for Fr. Patrick. May God's love bring healing for our son, Justin. We love you, Fr. Pat!

Buehler, Neil and Julie, Belmont, MI

If only we could all carry our cross as you do, Father Pat!

Burr, Viola, Hamilton, ONT, CANADA

Viola Burr

Butler, Barbara, Springfield, IL

Kenneth Butler

Butson, Janet, Blairsville, GA

In memory of my husband, Al

Cartwright, RN, Ann Marie, Floral Park, NY

Thank you, Fr. Pat, for your inspiration

Casey, Mr. and Mrs. Larry, Blairsville, GA

In thanksgiving for our eleven children

Chaffin, Mary, and Jerry Rivas, San Antonio, TX

In memory of deceased Chaffin and Rivas family members

Charlesworth, Ruth and Bob, Punta Gorda, FL

Our parents: Ruth and Frank, Theresa and Ferris

Childers and Family, Mr. and Mrs. Robert R., Fort Lauderdale, FL

In memory of Chuck

Christensen, Kenneth and Anita, El Campo, TX

To end abortion

Christensen, Kenneth and Anita , El Campo, TX

In memory of deceased family members

Cilli, Jane, Rumford, RI

With love and prayers from New Hope Prayer Group, Cumberland, RI

Coakley, Jim and Doris, Oxford, OH

In thanksgiving

Cohen and Family, Marty and Irene, Jackson, NJ

Since the day that you were an integral part of our being baptized Catholic to marrying two of our children, you'll never know how much you have impacted our lives and how much we love you for it! Hugs, Marty and Irene Cohen

Cole, Joyce, Springfield, IL

In memory of Dale Cole

Conlon, Sandra L., Springfield, IL

In thanksgiving

Connors, Mrs. Connie, Haverhill, MA

In memory of John and Bunny Connors

Connors, Joanne, Haverhill, MA

In memory of my dad, John Connors, and sister Bunny Connors

Connors, Kelly and Bob, Atkinson, NH

We dedicate this to all touched by Fr. Pat's words

Connors, MaryLou, Haverhill, MA

In honor of my brothers and sisters, who I love dearly

Connors, Richard T., Haverhill, MA

For Fr. Pat's great ministry

Cross, Judge Kelly M., Probate Court No. 1, San Antonio, TX

In thanksgiving

Cudak, Mr. and Mrs. Francis, Plainville, CT

In memory of our daughter, Heidi Velazquez and Jasmine

Cuyler, Wesley, Davie, FL

Wesley Cuyler Jr. and Robert L. Poirier

Davies, Sara L., West Palm Beach, FL

In memory of Bill Davies

De Leon, Roland and Monica, D'Hanis, TX

In memory of our grandparents

De Rosa, Jim and Iris, Murphy, NC

In thanksgiving for God's love

De Vera, Calvin and Linda, Honolulu, HI

In thanksgiving

Deguer, Christina, Weston, FL

Thank you!

Dercole, Sandra, Cranston, RI

In thanksgiving

Desaulniers and Family, Marty and Marie, Winnipeg, MB, CANADA

In thanksgiving and loving memory for all our family

Di Mattia, Virginia M., Providence, RI

My grandson, Dominick, and Nicholas Di Mattia: May they be blessed/grow into men of faith and character

Dietz, Don Paul and Janice, Morganton, GA

In thanksgiving

Downeast Flowers, Sanford, ME

In thanksgiving

Duval, Ray and Eileen, Wauregan, CT

In thanksgiving

Eichenholz, Sally, San Antonio, TX

In thanksgiving for my children and grandchildren

Evelo, Michael and Sheryl, Rhinelander, WI

In memory of John and Lorraine Evelo

Fantz, Birdie, Moore, TX

God's blessings for my niece Tammy, today, tomorrow, and forever

Faraone, Joseph, Cranston, RI

In thanksgiving

Fazzini, Noreen, Donora, PA

In thanksgiving

Filek, Jeanne, Franklin, CT

Good health, love, and peace for my three daughters

Finn, N , Belchertown, MA

In thanksgiving

Fiumano, Mr. and Mrs. Daniel, Young Harris, GA

Is. 40:31

Flood, Carolyn, Scottsdale, AZ

On behalf of Carl Flood

Flood, Mary Carla, Washington, D.C.

In memory of Marie and Bill Flood

Foley, Joyce, New York, NY

In thanksgiving

Fortier, Helene, Biddeford, ME

I thank God for my precious grandsons

Fortin, Collette, Fall River, MA

In memory of my parents for their loving kindness

Fournier, Helen and Marc, Biddeford, ME

In thanksgiving

Fox, Deacon Tom and Mary Jane, San Antonio, TX

In thanksgiving

Fritz, Adelina, San Antonio, TX

To Adelina and family

Gallagher, Judy, Anaconda, MT

In thanksgiving

Garcia, Jeri, Palacios, TX

In memory of "Pops." Love you!

Garcia, Elidia, Camarilla, CA

For all the farm and my family

Garcia-Aboytes, Charolette J., San Antonio, TX

Victor Aboytes

Gaucher, Mr. and Mrs. Ronald E., Hiawassee, GA

In dedication to our deceased parents

Geringer, Sister Agnes Marie, St. Clare's Villa, Alton, IL

In thanksgiving

Giard, Kim and Bruce, Stafford Springs, CT

In thanksgiving

Gombar, Elena and Jim, Weston, FL

In peace and love

Gonzales, Maryalvin, Peoria, AZ

Gonzalez, Dawn and Daniel, Freeville, NY

To the loving Gonzalez family

Graff, Tyler and Kelly, Hondo, TX

In honor of our parents

Graham, Mary, Rosedale, NY

In thanksgiving

Greeno, Jeanne, Wakefield, MA

In thanksgiving

Grizio, Margret and Myron, Hiawassee, GA

In thanksgiving for the many blessings received

Gross, Annette and Brandon, MB, CANADA

Faith, health, peace

Gross, Beatrice and Brandon, MB, CANADA

In gratitude for Father Patrick A. Martin

Gumaskas, Pete, Inverness, FL

In thanksgiving

Gurecky, Ed and Diana, Bay City, TX

In memory of Sister Eileen Gurecky

Gustafson, Marilyn, Springfield, IL

In memory of Paul Gustafson and Marjorie Rechner

Habedank, Lisa, Corapolis, PA

In memory of my beloved mom, Betty Bisson, and my two children, Kyle and Amanda

Haley, Susan Rousseau , Murphy, NC

In gratitude for Fr. Pat's introduction to God

Halm, Peg, W. Franklin, NH

In thanksgiving

Hawkins, Ken and Bobbie, Angels with Crooked Haloes and Wings, Phoenix, AZ

In thanksgiving for the healing, health, and happiness of our dear and precious Fr. Pat!

Hawkins, Mark, Glendale, AZ

Love and grateful thanksgiving from your Arizona IT guy, Mark

Hawkins and Family, Traci and Michael, Peoria, AZ

"Comparison is the thief of joy." Thank you, Fr. Pat, for teaching us to see God's love for each of us today.

Haynes, Steve and Eileen, Torrington, CT

In thanksgiving

Heilman, Mae Marie, Garden Grove, CA

Loving memory of Pauline MacDougall

Hermanson, Lou and Dolores, Inverness, FL

Memory of our grandson Mikie

Herrmann, Paul and Wanda, San Antonio, FL

Joe and Rose Herrmann

Hickl, Edith, El Maton, TX

In loving memory of my husband, Lawrence, and in thanksgiving of my children and their families

Hogan, Theresa, New York, NY

In thanksgiving

Holland, George and Cecilia, Blairsville, GA

In memory of my father, Norbert

Hopper, Virginia, New York, NY

In memory of Donald A. Hopper

Hopper, Ms. Justine, New York, New York

In loving memory of my dad, Donald Hopper (6/13/25–3/20/04)

Hormillosa, Erlinda, Hamilton, ONT, CANADA

For my son Christopher and his family

Hover, George and Patti, Colleyville, TX

Jesus we trust in you

Hunt, Susan, Kevin and Jack, Phoenix, AZ

Thank you, fantastic Fr. Pat, for living a life that inspires others

Hurta, Marvin and Wyonna, Palacios, TX

In thanksgiving for fifty-plus years of marriage

Jarvis, Sheila, Cumberland, RI

To Mark and Jared

Jepson, Lori, Killdeer, ND

For my husband, Loren

Jones, Julia, Coventry, RI

In thanksgiving

Kalinowski, Peter, Paso Robles, CA

In thanksgiving

Kavanagh, Susan, Falmouth, MA

In thanksgiving

Kelley, Eugenia, Richardton, ND

In honor of my mother, Charlotte Lane, who passed away on June 19, 2015

Kelley, Eugenia Lane, Richardton, ND

In memory of Charlotte Lane

Kenefick, Ana, Delray Beach, FL

In thanksgiving

Kerrigan and Family, Matthew and Barbara, Paso Robles, CA

In prayer and thanksgiving for our children: Katherine, Mary, Sean, Kevin, Teresa, and Sarah

Keyser, Dolores (Dee), Charles Town, WV

In memory of husband, Roger, and son, Mark

Kimball, Marguiritte W., Hiawassee, GA

In thanksgiving for blessings

Knutson, Kristi, Dunn Center, ND

To my mom and dad, with endless gratitude and love

Konow, Ida, Lehigh Acres, FL

Memory of my father, Stephen J. Konow

Kozar, Chuck, Monessen, PA

In thanksgiving

Kozar, Charles "Pete," Donora, PA

In loving memory of my wife, Joann Koza, and Aunt Kay

Kozar, Andrew, San Antonio, TX

I love my "Uncle Patrick"

Kozar, Jerome and Pat, San Antonio, TX

With love from his sister Patricia and "brother" Jerry

Krier, Linda, Santa Maria, CA

Thanks to God for his mercy

Kubicek, Joseph and Donnine, Turtletown, TN

In memory of Rudolph and Elizabeth Kubicek and Donald and Lola Tomas

Kumar, Rita, Minneola, NY

In Memory of mom, Joyce Kumar

La Fleche, Agnes and Sylvio, Ile Des Chenes, MB, CANADA

To the Sylvio and Agnes La Fleche family

LaMontagne, Bruce and Patty, Blairsville, GA

In memory of our parents Henry, Pat, Tom, and Nzla

Langfield, Mrs. Joan Theresa, D'Hanis, TX

In memory of my husband, Joseph C. Langfield, and my two sisters, Carolyn Ney and Terry Schueling

LaPorte, Mrs. Jeannette, Hollywood, FL

Dear Sister Connie Brochu

Lariviere, Rita, Norwich, CT

In memory of Jean L. Lariviere

LaRocca, Mr. and Mrs. Paul, Pembroke Pines, FL

Special intentions for our friend, Father Pat. You are amazing!

Lasseter, Anna, Zenny Sardinas, and Elsie Schrieffer, Davie, FL

Mantle of Love and Prayer Group

Leturmy, Larry and Pam, Murphy, NC

In honor of our grandchildren: Nicholas, Rachel, Sarah, and Gabriella

Levy, Barry, Methuen, MA

In memory of John Connors. You will always be remembered.

Lisk, Mr. and Mrs. Donald, Freeville, NY

In thanksgiving for our four children and in memory of our family and friends

Luther, Dana K., Andrews, NC

Thanks to Fr. Alex

Lutz, Louis and Mary Ann, D'Hanis, TX

In memory of our parents

Lynch, Mr. and Mrs. Raymond, Lawrence, MA

In thanksgiving

Lynch, Theresa, College Point, NY

In thanksgiving

MacLean, Pat, Winchester, BC, CANADA

In loving memory of my husband, James MacLean, deceased July 30, 2016

Magnificat Our Lady of Divine Providence Chapter, Cumberland, RI

Blessings from Linda and the RI Magnificat Team

Maher, Virginia and Robert, N. Providence, RI

Best wishes, Fr. Pat!

Mantle of Love Prayer Group, Plantation, FL

Dedicated to prayer group members

Mark, Maggie and Sara, Murphy, NC

Sara March Angel Outreach

Marotto, Camie and Ray, Cranston, RI

Consecration of our children and grandchildren to the sacred heart of Jesus and the immaculate heart of Mary

Martin, Mary, Rockledge, FL

In memory of his brother Reginald W. Martin

Martin, Mabel, Sherman, IL

My husband Mike, my grandchildren, and my family

Martinez, Ricardo and Diana, San Antonio, TX

For Celeste and Carmen

Mathieu, Bob and Priscilla, Biddeford, ME

In thanksgiving

Matulis, Robert, Greensboro, NC

In thanksgiving

McCauley, Anne and Andrew, Weston, FL

You are an inspiration to everyone who crosses your path.
God bless you!

Mercade Family, Port St. Lucie, FL

In thanksgiving

Merlino, Dr. Anthony, North Providence, RI

In loving memory of Dolores Merlino

Mertz and Family, Madeline, Bainbridge, NY

Dedicated to the family

Metscher, Ann, Dania Beach, FL

In thanksgiving

Metzger, Francis, Young Harris, GA

Francis from Francis

Michael, Mr. and Mrs. Mason, Amherst, NY

In thanksgiving

Michael, Jerry Bisson and Barbara, Blairsville, GA

In memory of Bisson and Michael families

Moncada, Lucy, D'Hanis, TX

In memory of my father, Carlos Muniz

Mondo, Mary Ann, Pembroke Pines, FL

In memory of Joe Mondo

Morris, Ernie and Dorothy, San Antonio, TX

In memory of Richard Morris

Mueller, Fred and Maria, Satellite Beach, FL

Happiness is helping to spread the Word

Muklewicz, Karen, Woodhaven, MI

In memory of my husband, Tony Muklewicz

Muklewicz, Karen, Woodhaven, MI

In memory of baby Faith

Myers, Nancy A., Taylor, MI

In memory of my dear son, Jimmy Myers

Nelan, Rev. Kevin J., New York, NY

God bless Father Patrick

Newport, Jacqueline, Biddeford, ME

In thanksgiving

Nguyen, Tai, Garden Grove, CA

In thanksgiving

Ontiveros, Sylvia, Yancey, TX

Giving thanks to God that my son, Jacob, has found the Lord!

Paquette, Jen and Serge, 2432 31 St. SW, MB, CANADA

For all the Paquetts, Smiths, Bryants, and Devlins

Parrow, Maureen, Anaconda, MT

In memory of my daughter Jennifer

Pearce, Dick and Nancy, Wauchula, FL

In loving memory of our deceased family members

Pelletier and Family, Jack and Susan, Fort Lauderdale, FL

Jack and Susan Pelletier and family

Peterson, Beatrice, San Antonio, TX

In thanksgiving

Petronio, Joanne and Pat, Smithfield, RI

Peace and God's love in the hearts of our family

Piotrowski, Jeanne and Chuck, Port Sanilal, MI

In thanksgiving

Plante, Larry and Mary, Berlin, CT

Wish Fr. Pat for continued good health

Pollack, Marie, Groton, NY

In thanksgiving

Prendergast, Edmond, Davie, FI,

In thanksgiving

Priest, James and Maria, Blairsville, GA

In thanksgiving for my husband

Pupke, Ruth, New York, NY

To Joe Gaynor, a light in the darkness

Quistorff, James A., Murphy, NC

In thanksgiving for Gayle's conversion

Ranieri, Patrick, Indian Harbour Beach, FL

May our Lord Jesus bless my Mary with his eternal life!

Rechner, Bill and Donna, Springfield, IL

In memory of Fran Schwartz, a great friend, faithful rosary-maker, and world-class peanut-brittle maker

Rechner, Bill and Donna, Springfield, IL

In thanksgiving

Rechner, Keith E., Springfield, IL

Fr. Luigi Evangelisto: Grüss Gott

Rechner, Keith E., Springfield, IL

In memory of Robin Webster

Reyes, Ralph, Vicky, Sydney, Sierra, and Secilia, D'Hanis, TX

In memory of Ben O. Reyes

Ricchiazzi, Tony and Diane, Belchertown, MA

Ricchiazzi and Supczak families

Ripper, Maureen, Murphy, NC

The Ripper family

Robinson, Margaret Ann, Sault Ste. Marie, ONT, CANADA

My daughter, Stephanie, and her husband, George

Rodriguez, Irene, Garden Grove, CA

In memory of my mother, Irene P. Zuñga

Rohde, Bill and Evelyn, Groton, NY

In memory of our son Jeffrey Rohde

Romanelli, Anita, Jenny Martino, N. Providence, RI

In thanksgiving for Fr. Pat, our families, and friends

Romjurad, George, Westminster, CA

In thanksgiving

Rondon, Michele, Uniondale, NY

In thanksgiving

Rothe, Susie, D'Hanis, TX

In thanksgiving for my three blessings: Jenny Sue, Michel Thomas, and J'Lynn Michaela

Rousseau, Lucien and Madeline, Blairsville, GA

In memory of the Franciscan Martyrs of Siroki Brijed

Ruus and Family, Rauno and Corina, Ile des Chenes East, MB, CANADA

To our parents, Larry and Elaine, Martta, Barry and Joan, and our grandparents, Vern and Iva and Desire and Selvie

Ryan, John, Hampton Bays, NY

In thanksgiving

Sbardella, Richard and Lynn, Stafford Springs, CT

In memory of our parents

Schultz, James and Kathleen, Murphy, NC

Thanksgiving for sons and daughters, grandkids, and great-grandkids

Schulz, Susan A., Ft. Lauderdale, FL

In thanksgiving for the priesthood of Father John McLaughlin, Father Tony Mulderry, and Father Fritzner Bellonce

Schwarz, Bob and Gloria, Highland, IL

Continued success of Fr. Pat's missions and good health

Scioli, Janet and Michael, Rockledge, FL

In memory of our parents, Michael and Laura Scioli and Wilfred and Mary Thomas

Sealy, Linda and Ted, Wakefield, RI

Edward and Gloria Sealy, Ben and Ida Faraone

Sens, Bernie and Carole, Oxford, OH

Fantastic, he loves us.

Shaulys, Gwen, Hicksville, NY

The Shaulys family

Shewchuk, Joanne and Frank, Kitchener, ONT, CANADA

Continued blessings on Father Pat's missions

Shortell, Mary, and Therese Harnois, Ansonia, CT

You continue to be God's instrument that shows us his love!

Sikora, Richard, Taylor, MI

In thanksgiving for my wonderful wife and marriage

Simard, Lucille T., Saco, ME

To Mom and Dad: Marc and Antoinette Simard

Slentz, Bill and DeDe, W. Melbourne, FL

Shewchuk, Joanne and Frank, Kitchener, ONT, CANADA

Continued blessings on Father Pat's missions

Smith, Guy and Eileen, Brandon, MB, CANADA

For our children and their loved ones. We love you, F.P.!

Smith, Richard and Michelle, Murphy, NC

In honor for Stephanie Ambrosio

Smith, Scott and Veronica, Delray Beach, FL

For the poor at heart, that God enrich their lives

Smith, Richard and Michelle, Murphy, NC

In honor for Stephanie Ambrosio

Solis, Rene and Jim, Brasstown, NC

In thanksgiving for James P. Solis III

Soliz, Domingo, Palacios, TX

Sommers, Bud and Barbara, Murphy, NC

In honor of Louis and Toni Altier

Soto, Miriam, Fort Lauderdale, FL

Stabler, Mr. and Mrs. Richard, Stratford, CT

Taglioli, Joe and Debbie, Inkster, MI

In thanksgiving for AA in our lives

Teetaert, Larry and Elaine, Deloraine, MB, CANADA

In memory of "Mom's" passing, Sept. 22, 2016: "RIP Sylvia"

Teetaert, Murray and Adrienne, MB, CANADA

In loving memory of our brother, Maurice Teetaert, and mom, Selvie Missinne

Thompson, Eloise, Keller, TX

Honor of Sara March, who taught me about God's love

Torres, Susana, Weston, FL

In thanksgiving

Tyler, June, Blairsville, GA

To my parents

Vachon and Family, Albert and Anita, Albuquerque, NM

In thanksgiving

Van Buskirk, Brian and Annalyn, Andrews, NC

Honor of my daughter LeAnn V.

Vanasse, Paul and Donna, Belchertown, MA

In memory of our parents

Vassallo, Marilyn A., Mantoloking, NJ

Love you and your work

Vidya, Jai and Alex, Bryn Mawr, PA

Please pray for John, Desh, Alex, and Grace

Villanueva, Eloy Saenz and Gloria, Boerne, TX

We love you, Fr. Pat.

Vinton, Eloise, Oxnard, CA

To Eloise

Vivion, Tom and Barbara, Blessing, TX

In thanksgiving

Wall, Audrey, Miami Shores, FL

In honor of Anna M. Little

Wallace, John and Anne, Locust Valley, NY

To our children that they will always feel God's love through their lives

Walsh, Joyce, Freeville, NY

In memory of my husband, Charles Walsh

Watson, Wayne and Karen, Hayesville, NC

Dedicated to our children and grandchildren

Wiesner, Peter and Fran, Mount Hope, ONT, CANADA

In thanksgiving

White, Sylvia M., Weston, ME

In thanksgiving

Williams, Mrs. Marie, Waterville, ME

You go, Uncle Pat

Williams, Pat, Hiawassee, GA

In memory of my mother

Wise, Mr. and Mrs. Robert L., Springfield, IL

Thank you for loving thoughts and inspiration

Wise, Robert and Helen, Springfield, IL

Thank you, Jesus, for the gift of Fr. Pat's inspired message from Jesus

Wise, Robert and Helen, Springfield, IL

God bless our children

Wise, Robert and Helen, Springfield, IL

In thanksgiving for the many blessings Jesus sends our family and friends

Wood, Patsy, Caribou, ME

In loving memory of John F. Wood by wife and family

Young, Ray and Marie, Indialantic, FL

In memory of Brice Chestnut

THANK YOU! THANK YOU! THANK YOU!

CPSIA information can be obtained
at www.ICGtesting.com
Printed in the USA
FSHW022125010319